If the Scriptures have not grasp[...] sermon is unlikely to say anything [...] the preacher has not been involve[...] and personal involvement, they [...] her. So this work on imaginative engagement with the Scriptures might be the most important book that many preachers read, apart from the Scriptures into which it leads them.

John Goldingay
David Allan Hubbard Professor of Old Testament, School of Theology,
Fuller Theological Seminary, Pasadena, USA

I am drawn to any exposition of "imagination" in the practice of faith. This remarkable volume focuses on imagination, but sets it squarely in the midst of the great triad of pastor-prayer-congregation. This is pastoral theology at its best, inviting pastors and church leaders to let the power of the Spirit – via the generative force of Scripture – to be in defining play in ministry. Coming close to articulating "how to," this book will challenge and engage pastoral leadership in a sense of immense risk and opportunity. "Imagination," it turns out, is openness to the Spirit and being led by a spirit other than our own. The invitation of this book is warmly companionable.

Walter Brueggemann
Columbia Theological Seminary, Decatur, USA

I was fascinated by the research reported by this book, *Imaginative Preaching*, and have already started to put it into practice. Preachers all over the world would benefit profoundly if they cultivated these prayer disciplines to rekindle their love for God, deepen their immersion in the Scriptures, and rejuvenate their love and affection for the people whom they serve! A sublime idea!

Marva J. Dawn
Theologian, Author, Preacher and Speaker

Jesus' disciples watched him pray and then pleaded: "Lord, teach us to pray . . ." (Luke 11:1). Jesus did so and also invited them to imagine that God, like a friend in the night, offers them bread when they ask for it. This book offers a similar assurance of God's grace and imaginative prayer as a means of receiving that grace. Through careful research and reflection, pastor-scholar Geoff New introduces road-tested Christian practices of praying with Scripture so that depleted souls may be refreshed by the Bread of Life and bear fruit in the world. Dr New's invitation to imaginative prayer with Scripture is a gift I gratefully accept for myself and also share with Christians, clergy and laity that I meet with in spiritual direction. The blessings flow!

Susan S. Phillips
Executive Director of New College Berkeley,
Berkeley Graduate Theological Union, Berkeley, USA
Author of *Candlelight: Illuminating the Art of Spiritual Direction* and
The Cultivated Life: From Ceaseless Striving to Receiving Joy

How can preachers encounter the risen Christ in ways that make preaching fresh, real and accessible? How can preachers grow in dwelling in Christ and dwelling in the Word? Geoff New presents a powerful and helpful model for meeting God personally through the words of the biblical text, vitally important for authentic preaching in our time.

Lynne M. Baab
author of *Sabbath Keeping* and *The Power of Listening*

Global Perspectives Series

Imaginative Preaching

Langham
GLOBAL LIBRARY

Imaginative Preaching

*Praying the Scriptures so
God Can Speak through You*

Geoff New

Langham

GLOBAL LIBRARY

© 2015 by Geoff New

Published 2015 by Langham Global Library
an imprint of Langham Creative Projects

Langham Partnership
PO Box 296, Carlisle, Cumbria CA3 9WZ, UK
www.langham.org

ISBNs:
978-1-78368-899-9 Print
978-1-78368-877-7 Mobi
978-1-78368-878-4 ePub
978-1-78368-876-0 PDF

British Library Cataloguing in Publication Data

New, Geoff, author.
  Imaginative preaching : praying the Scriptures so God can
  speak through you.
  1. Preaching. 2. Prayer--Christianity. 3. Bible--
  Devotional use. 4. Contemplation. 5. Spiritual exercises.
  I. Title
  251-dc23

ISBN-13: 9781783688999

Cover & Book Design: projectluz.com

Contents

Abstract

This research examines the effect of utilizing two ancient prayer disciplines, *lectio divina* and Ignatian Gospel Contemplation, as part of regular sermon preparation. A group of eight ministers and pastors, including the author of this work, committed to using both prayer disciplines during a four-month period in 2010. During this time, *lectio divina* and Ignatian Gospel Contemplation were integrated with the preachers' normal rhythm of exegetical and theological preparation for the text at hand. The group members met regularly and their reflections and action were facilitated by an action-research model.

This research was a response to a long-standing and widespread call for the use of the imagination in preaching, a call which is marked by an associated lament at the lack of progress in preaching in this regard. Connected with the lack of imagination, and to some extent the reason for it, are the intense demands of pastoral ministry and the struggle experienced by the preacher-pastor to engage personally with the Scriptures in preparation for their public exposition. Chapter 1 discusses the imagination in relation to the Scriptures and preaching. Chapter 2 explains and describes the two prayer disciplines. Appendix B outlines the research method employed for this research exercise.

As a result of the engagement with the two ancient prayer disciplines, ten major themes emerged. These themes clustered naturally into three areas which form three chapters discussing the findings (chs. 3 to 5). The three clusters of themes cover:

- A sobering discovery of the preacher's state in relation to their call to preach, the growth of a sense of personal authenticity and a renewed relationship with the Scriptures.
- The struggles and triumphs of wrestling with the text as a result of the prayer disciplines. This includes the issue of which personal encounters, experienced during prayer, warranted public expression in the sermon and the positive discoveries which aided that discernment process.
- The enrichment of the connection with the congregation, the emergence of an expansion of the imagination and the impact of the two prayer disciplines on wider ministry activities.

The thesis concludes in chapter 6, where the findings of the research are summarized through the lens of the account of the disciples on the road to Emmaus (Luke 24:13–35).

Acknowledgements

The oft-quoted African proverb "It takes a village to raise a child" sums up the process of writing this book. It was a community event and is smudged with the community's fingerprints.

Rev Dr Lynne Baab – my supervisor. Your thoroughness, insight and skill are matched only by the warmth of your pastoral heart and your patience with my use of semi-colons. Thank you for your guidance and empowerment over the past two years.

The group participants – the Magnificent Seven. It seems wrong that I cannot name you, but given that you are referred to by pseudonyms in this book I am bound to keep to that here. You opened yourselves up to this research by opening yourselves up to the work of the Spirit. You displayed an extraordinary level of vulnerability and humility in your preaching and in pouring your hearts and souls into our discussions and reflections. You are the heroes and heroines of this research. Any benefit that the church derives from this exercise is due to your sacrifice and courage. May you know the pleasure of the Head of the church and his reward kept for you in heaven (Matt 6:6; 1 Pet 1:3–5).

Papakura East and Hunua Presbyterian Church – to faithful people of God in this church who have allowed their minister to explore, innovate, imagine, trial and experiment in their midst. And you kept coming back for more and continued to encourage me in it all. May the Word continue to dwell richly in your hearts (Col 3:16).

Dr David Crawley – my spiritual director. "Gift" is the word I use to describe you. You are a gift from God and you gifted me regular insights, resources and counsel throughout.

Rev John Fairbrother, and the board and staff of Vaughan Park Anglican Retreat Centre – your gift of three months' residency to study was literally life-changing. The space you created, nurtured and protected was profound. The discernment and sensitivity accorded to me during my stay was christlike. Few things in life exceed expectations – but your scholarship programme is out of this world and a foretaste of heaven!

Anne Aalbers – registrar at Laidlaw-Carey Graduate School. Thank you for your kindness, efficiency, good humour and efforts to smooth the way.

Thank you too for your warm and robust engagement with my thesis content. You strengthened it.

Dr Christine Woods – of how many serendipitous moments have you been the agent during my years studying? Thank you for saying the right thing at the right time – so often! Thank you too for your passion for learning. It's contagious.

Rev Dr Paul Windsor – thank you for your influence, and for helping to crystallize my thesis topic. Thank you too for your dedication to advancing preaching the world over, and for the freshness and originality with which you do so. Your gift in being able to read the Word of God and the spirit of the age is profound. Thank you mostly for your friendship.

Rev Dr Carolyn Kelly – one of the most extraordinary people I have the privilege of calling "friend." Thank you for introducing me to two of your friends – George MacDonald and Hans Urs von Balthasar – even though you knew you were tossing me a live hand grenade with one of them! But truly I am in your debt. Thank you too for your powerful paraphrasing which enabled me to understand what I meant.

Rev Dr Paul Prestidge – our friendship, especially during this period of study, has been one of my best memories. Your sharp intellect, your ability to see clearly and your good humour have been a form of true north for me.

Rev Canon Sue Burns – thank you for the way in which you orientated me to important issues and people very early on. At a time when it was not easy to know exactly where to start, you provided much-needed direction and encouragement.

Fr Stuart Sellar – in the very early days of my research you were instrumental in gifting me momentum and confidence. That afternoon at the Good Shepherd College, when you generously gave me unhurried time and opened up so much to me, will stay long in my memory. Your advice and encouragement were heaven-sent.

Fr John O'Connor – thank you for two hours of possibly the most unnerving, unsettling and yet empowering conversation I can recall. You helped me plumb and define what was important and what was superfluous.

Tim Jollie – for your generous encouragement and provision of funds from the CAT Trust. You worked hard to remove any sense of embarrassment concerning finances and garnished that with regular and warm encouragement.

Rev Dr Doug Lendrum (Nellie Inglis Trust) – thank you for your regular and generous support. You always pleasantly surprised me with your grants. It made the difference!

Knox Centre for Ministry and Leadership – thank you for your financial support, and for your encouragement and enablement for ministers to maintain an edge and keep fresh.

Margaret van Ginkel – for your unbelievable powers of observation when proofreading. Thank you for your thoroughness.

Josiah New – to my son who, while at breakfast at McDonald's, said just the right thing to launch me on the DMin journey. At a time when I was struggling with the decision and uncertain about its implications, you were prophetic. That conversation remains vibrant and treasured. I hope I can make you proud.

Luke New – to my son who experienced all the absences as I attended to my study – yet never complained. In fact, you sent me back to study regularly with the loaded question "Aren't you studying today?" Thanks for allowing me short breaks on PlayStation and Xbox.

James & Rebekah Nimmo – to my son-in-law and daughter, you both have a wonderful combination of a calm demeanour shot through with a joy and zest for life. Even though geographically we are apart, your effect has been close to home and has strengthened me.

Ruth New – my wife. You personify your biblical namesake. Your loyalty to me, and belief in me, is a gift from God. Simply put, this book would not have happened but for you. To borrow Joseph Choate's tribute to his wife: "If I died and was able to come back as anyone I liked – it would be as your second husband."

Introduction

If the preachers of this world had only one passage with which to study and preach, Hebrews 1:1–4 would powerfully demonstrate the exhilaration and agony which accompany such a ministry.[1] How can a preacher in the twenty-first century convey to their congregation a legitimate sense of connection with their biblical heritage? Will God speak through this sermon? How can the revelation of Hebrews 1:1–4 be handled, and what are its implications? Congregations expect an answer to these questions every week. The problem of preaching can be put thus:

- Is God willing to speak through preaching, but not able? Then we are left impotent.
- Is he able, but not willing? Then we are left with a malevolent God.
- Is he both able and willing? Whence then is the struggle?[2]

Both the biblical record and Christian experience attest to the ability and willingness of God to speak to his people. Yet confounding such divine readiness is a struggle experienced by preachers as they endeavour to expound the Scriptures and mediate his Word and voice. In response to this problem, this research project explores the effect of utilizing two contemplative approaches of engaging with Scripture – *lectio divina* and Ignatian Gospel Contemplation – as part of routine sermon preparation and in conjunction with the best of historical-critical exegesis in preaching. While the struggle to facilitate the message of God through preaching can be due to a myriad of issues, three will suffice by way of introduction to this work. Each of the issues is accompanied by a corresponding hypothesis.

---

1. "Long ago God spoke to our ancestors in many and various ways by the prophets, but in these last days he has spoken to us by a Son, whom he appointed heir of all things, through whom he also created the worlds. He is the reflection of God's glory and the exact imprint of God's very being, and he sustains all things by his powerful word. When he had made purification for sins, he sat down at the right hand of the Majesty on high, having become as much superior to angels as the name he has inherited is more excellent than theirs" (Heb 1:1–4 NRSV). All Bible references are from NRSV.

2. This is a play on eighteenth-century David Hume's famous formula concerning God and the problem of evil: "Is he willing to prevent evil, but not able? Then he is impotent. Is he able, but not willing? Then he is malevolent. Is he both able and willing? Whence then is evil?" Quoted in J. Millard Erikson, *Christian Theology* (Grand Rapids: Baker, 1985), 412.

- **Problem 1:** The demands of pastoral ministry compete for the preacher's time and attention to the Scriptures.
- **First hypothesis:** *Lectio divina* and Ignatian Gospel Contemplation orientate preachers to a primary relationship with Scripture

The attractiveness of *lectio divina* and Ignatian Gospel Contemplation is that they assume the primacy of Scripture and the significance of the incarnation. Through concentrated reading and praying of the text the preacher is positioned to receive the Word of God today for the life of discipleship. The preacher is thereby placed in the position of Samuel (1 Sam 3:9–10) and of Mary (Luke 1:38) as an expectant recipient. The reason for advancing *lectio divina* and Ignatian Gospel Contemplation is not to suggest that preachers do not pray and study when preparing sermons, but to acknowledge the ever-present struggle to avoid deep engagement with the text, resulting in sermons which are either superficial or too academic. Compounding this struggle, pastoral demands compete with the regular deadline to prepare a sermon. In the preacher's effort to attend to ministry outside the pulpit, sermon preparation founded on the study of the Scriptures can become a casualty. Nieman describes the issue thus:

> As the pressures of parish life mount and the "urgent" supplants what is genuinely important, we say, "Well, it won't hurt if just *this* week I don't spend quite as much time on sermon preparation." And lo and behold, we were absolutely right! They love us anyway! "Good sermon," they continue to chime at the door. Week by week we learn to get by with less and less text study, prayer, and reflection.[3]

Hence the primacy of Scripture in the life of the church is eroded. Alternatively, in the sincere attempt to give due attention to sermon preparation and to honour one's training in exegesis, the sermon can become too cerebral and is removed from the lives of the listeners. The preacher becomes divorced from pastoral contact, so the wry observation "that only the preacher comes to church with a burning interest in the Jebusites"[4]

---

3. James R. Nieman, "Preaching That Drives People from the Church," in *A Reader on Preaching: Making Connections*, ed. David Day, Jeff Astley and Leslie J. Francis (Aldershot: Ashgate, 2005), 248 (emphasis in original).

4. Fosdick quoted in Richard Lischer, "Imagining a Sermon," in *A Reader on Preaching: Making Connections*, ed. David Day, Jeff Astley and Leslie J. Francis (Aldershot: Ashgate, 2005), 182.

becomes a mind-numbing reality. In the light of the incarnation, preachers are honour-bound to embody the reality of the Word made flesh and not give their congregations reason to think that their pastors are in the pay of the chief priests trying to keep the reason for the empty tomb a secret.

- **Problem 2:** The preacher remains unmoved by Scripture.
- **Second hypothesis:** *Lectio divina* and Ignatian Gospel Contemplation facilitate the growth of the preacher's authenticity.

In 1877, Phillips Brooks offered a definition of preaching which has served as a poignant point of reference ever since: "Truth through personality."[5] However, in practice preachers can consign "truth" to the period of preparation and "personality" to the time of delivery without the two truly coming into contact. Consequently, the integrity of the text and the authenticity of the preacher are at best compromised and at worst fake. The separation of truth and personality erodes authenticity, especially if the previous observation concerning decreasing preparation with the Scriptures becomes habitual. A more comprehensive citation of Brooks' definition is helpful:

> Truth through personality is our description of real preaching. The truth must come really through the person, not merely over his lips, not merely into his understanding and out through his pen. It must come through his character, his affections, his whole intellectual and moral being. It must come genuinely through him.[6]

Truth and personality are inseparable, and attention to this dynamic enhances the authenticity of the preaching ministry. If the preacher suspends their personal involvement during the time of study, it follows that they will not be authentically present in the moment of delivery.

To bring Ignatian Gospel Contemplation to bear upon the Scripture at hand is to expose the preacher to intimacy with God and his love. Authenticity involves the realization of what it means to be human in the here and now:

> The essence of Ignatius' message was "Wake up!" The Application of the Senses [an Ignatian Prayer form] is about breathing. We are not breathing. We are not alive. Ignatius would say we draw on the five senses to be present. So that later, after prayer, we

---

5. Phillips Brooks, *Phillips Brooks on Preaching* (London: SPCK, 1965), 8.
6. Brooks, *Phillips Brooks on Preaching*, 8.

are present even to that person walking by whom we would otherwise dismiss or ignore.[7]

The effect of Ignatian Gospel Contemplation is to become more aware of God's mission and the world in which he calls us to serve. The genius of Ignatian prayer is to present the person with a transforming choice to find the will of God by being conformed to "the law of life laid down by Christ."[8] The possibility of such a response to God during sermon preparation sets up a tantalizing prospect for preaching. The practice of *lectio divina* presents the person with a similar encounter. *Lectio divina* is less of an approach to prayer than an expression of commitment to God; it is a lifestyle founded on the Scriptures and is not for those who shy away from having convictions, vision and approaches to life changed through the agency of prayer.[9] Authenticity relies on being shaped by Scripture, empowered by the Spirit of Christ and being genuinely available to God's call. "'The Word became flesh and dwelt among us . . . full of grace and truth' (John 1:14). That is what incarnation means. It is untheological. It is unsophisticated. It is undignified. But according to Christianity it is the way things are."[10] The struggle is to honour this through preaching in such a way that listeners are affirmed in their humanity and inspired to become Christlike.

- **Problem 3:** The preacher remains underwhelmed by the presence of God.
- **Third hypothesis:** *Lectio divina* and Ignatian Gospel Contemplation aid the recovery of imagination in preaching.

Imagination is a gift from God to enable humanity to discern his presence and work in this world. It operates as the clearing house in which the preacher is confronted with grace and revelation through a searching engagement with the written and incarnate Word. Imagination is the means by which preachers can be immersed in the Word during sermon preparation and in the act of preaching. However, some attempts to employ the imagination in preaching can be reduced to a game of "Let's Pretend."[11] Such attempts neglect sound exegesis, misappropriate the intent of Scripture and threaten the *raison d'être*

---

7. Fr John O'Connor, interview about Ignatian spirituality with the author, 2009.

8. Hugo Rahner, *Ignatius the Theologian* (New York: Herder & Herder, 1968), 55.

9. Michael Casey, *Sacred Reading: The Ancient Art of Lectio Divina* (Liguor: Triumph, 1996).

10. Frederick Buechner, *Wishful Thinking: A Theological ABC* (New York: Harper & Row, 1973), 43.

11. Lischer, "Imagining a Sermon," 181.

of preaching, which is to apply the meaning of the biblical story today with an eye on what God has promised for the future. The result has been a loss to theology in general, week-by-week preaching specifically, and the day-to-day discipleship of Christians particularly. Insofar as a vacuum of the imagination exists, a specific and terrible toll is exacted upon the ministry of preaching: a loss of wonder.

G. K. Chesterton puts the case succinctly: "The world will never starve for want of wonders, but only for want of wonder."[12] Even a cursory survey of the Bible demonstrates the centrality of wonder in the life and worship of the people of God. Psalm 8 records incredulity at the mindfulness of God towards humanity; Psalm 19 declares God's global and constant presence in creation; Psalm 139 expresses astonishment at the dimensions of God's attention; and Job's repentance (Job 42:1–7) is birthed from wonder. In the New Testament we see wonder at the birth narratives (Matt 2; Luke 2) and the post-resurrection occurrences (John 20). The day of Pentecost (Acts 2) is marked by the apostles declaring the wonders of God in foreign languages. The Epistles continue the theme in such passages as Colossians 1:15–20, which describes the supremacy of Christ; Ephesians 3:14–21, which translates such revelation into prayer; and Romans 11:33–36, which expresses it as a doxology. Wonder is the child of the imagination, and any absence of wonder in churches' lives points to a barren imagination. Gallagher[13] comments, "[W]e need to acknowledge the role of imagination as an alternative wavelength of knowing, a mode of alert wonder, more receptive than analytical in its method." *Lectio divina* and Ignatian Gospel Contemplation powerfully aid the preacher to tune into an "alternative wavelength of knowing." If preachers have not had their imaginations ignited by such divine reality and experienced true wonder at what God has accomplished through Christ, can they truly preach it? The value of *lectio divina* and Ignatian Gospel Contemplation is that they demand receptivity and humility which coach the imagination. Through their interaction with Scripture, they aid the imagination to enrich sermons so that people are better placed to live life according to the Scriptures. The call for the use of imagination in preaching is long-standing and widespread, and our attention now focuses on this appeal because it crystallizes and plumbs the

---

12. Quoted in Warren W. Wiersbe, *Preaching and Teaching with Imagination: The Quest for Biblical Ministry* (Grand Rapids: Baker, 1994), 69.

13. Michael Paul Gallagher, "Theology and Imagination: From Theory to Practice," *Christian Higher Education* 5 (2006): 83–96. Accessed 30 October 2009 at http://www.plaything.co.uk/gallagher/academic/theol_imag.html.

depths of much of the discussion pertaining to the struggles and challenges facing preaching today.

1

Imagination: Seeing the World as God Sees It and Intends It

In the first of a series of lectures at Yale University in 1871–1874, Henry Ward Beecher said, "The first element on which your preaching will largely depend for power and success, you will perhaps be surprised to learn, is *Imagination*, which I regard as the most important of all the elements that go to make the preacher."[1] G. Campbell Morgan complemented this with his contention that "imagination is the supreme work of [sermon] preparation."[2] Given the passage of time, it is prudent to consider whether such counsel has been heeded and if imagination is evident in preaching today. Burghardt provides an initial answer:

> In recent years I have argued that four problems prevent today's homily from being any better than yesterday's sermon: fear of Sacred Scripture, ignorance of contemporary theology, unawareness of liturgical prayer, and lack of proper preparation. The list has a lamentable lacuna. I have left out the most serious lack of all: imagination. Without imagination the preacher limps along on one leg.[3]

---

1. Henry Ward Beecher, "The Power of the Imagination," in *Developing a Christian Imagination: An Interpretative Anthology*, ed. Warren W. Wiersbe (Wheaton: Victor, 1995), 216, emphasis in original.

2. Quoted in David L. Larsen, *Telling the Old Old Story: The Art of Narrative Preaching* (Wheaton: Crossway, 1995), 241.

3. Walter J. Burghardt, *Preaching: The Art and the Craft* (New York: Paulist, 1987), 19.

Coupled with this, Peterson describes the legacy of a technological and "information-obsessed"[4] age. He writes, "A major and too-little-remarked evil in our time is the systematic degradation of the imagination. The imagination is among the chief glories of the human . . . Right now, one of the essential Christian ministries in and to our ruined world is the recovery and exercise of the imagination."[5] In the light of his challenge, this research proposes that the ministry of preaching is an important response to the dearth of imagination, given that the sermon is when most of the people of God are most often exposed to the effects of the study and application of the Scriptures.

This "systematic degradation of the imagination" was earlier identified by D. H. Lawrence, who wrote the following for a newspaper in October 1928:

> Now the great and fatal fruit of our civilization, which is a civilization based on knowledge, and hostile to experience, is boredom. All our wonderful education and learning is producing a grand sum total of boredom. They are bored because they experience nothing. And they experience nothing because the wonder has gone out of them. And when the wonder has gone out of a man he is dead.[6]

The unnerving questions which emerge are: is preaching today contributing to the "degradation of the imagination" or to the "recovery and exercise" of it? Is contemporary preaching part of the "grand sum total of boredom"? Is preaching today devoid of experience and therefore devoid of wonder? How can preaching become "one of the essential Christian ministries in and to our ruined world"? Insofar as Peterson's and Lawrence's comments are applicable to the practice of preaching, the answers to such questions are found in the way the Scriptures are handled in the preparation of sermons.[7] This chapter considers the place of the imagination and the exegetical historical-critical method in the formation of sermons.

The importance of Scripture in the formation of the church cannot be exaggerated, nor can the need for those Scriptures to be engaged with in healthy

---

4. Eugene H. Peterson, *Under the Unpredictable Plant: An Exploration in Vocational Holiness* (Grand Rapids: Eerdmans, 1992), 172.

5. Ibid., 171.

6. Quoted in Aelred Squire, *Asking the Fathers* (London: SPCK, 1973), 126.

7. It needs to be acknowledged that Peterson was writing specifically for Christian leadership and Lawrence was not. However, Lawrence's observation holds true insofar as professional Christian leaders are trained and educated for ministry, and various members of their congregations are educated for other capacities in life.

ways. The gospel of John begins with a dramatic formula and revelation of the incarnation: the divine Word becoming human flesh (John 1:1–5, 14). The Word of God is not simply ink and paper but flesh and bones. Since then, it has been incumbent upon the Christian church to study and interpret Scripture in sound and life-giving ways which honour the incarnation. In particular, the church has held the reasonable expectation that her leaders will study, present and apply Scripture in accurate, holistic, dynamic, relational and revelatory ways. This calls for sound exegesis and Spirit-guided imagination. Goldingay states, "We need to understand Scripture historically. But we also need to be open to leaps of inspired imagination."[8] To recover imagination in preaching means that "our sense of wonder, our God-given imagination, must in modern city life be consciously cultivated by whatever means are possible and authentic."[9]

An engaging and personally authentic study of Scripture is called for in the preparation of the sermon. Peterson puts the case strongly: "Is it time to get aggressive, time for Christian communities to recognize, honour, and commission its pastors as Masters of the Imagination, joining our poets, singers, and storytellers as partners in evangelical witness?"[10] With Peterson's call have come recent insightful contributions which provide some direction and context to embody a response. These include Steinmetz demonstrating unexpected similarities between Martin Luther and Ignatius of Loyola in their imaginative exegesis of Scripture for preaching;[11] Schneiders' observance of and appeal for Catholic spirituality and Protestant Bible-study techniques to converge;[12] Quicke's suggestion that preachers immerse themselves in Scripture by *lectio divina*;[13] Heisler's indebtedness to Haddon Robinson's

---

8. John Goldingay, "Premodern, Modern, and Postmodern in Old Testament Study," in James D. G. Dunn and John W. Rogerson, eds, *Eerdmans Commentary on the Bible* (Grand Rapids: Eerdmans, 2003), 19.

9. Squire, *Asking the Fathers*, 126.

10. Peterson, *Under the Unpredictable Plant*, 172.

11. "Perhaps the strongest similarity between Luther and Loyola lies in their common appeal to the human imagination as an instrument of spiritual nurture and reform. What links Luther to Loyola is their shared conviction that the reliving of the biblical story requires the full utilization of the powers of the human imagination. No flat, two-dimensional, cardboard characters for Luther or Loyola. The biblical narratives must be recaptured with all the life, vigour, colour, and emotional power of the original. Nothing less will do." David C. Steinmetz, "Luther and Loyola," *Interpretation* 47, no. 1 (1993), 12.

12. Sandra Schneiders, "Biblical Spirituality," *Interpretation* 56, no. 2 (2002): 133–142.

13. Michael Quicke, *360-Degree Preaching: Hearing, Speaking and Living the Word* (Grand Rapids: Baker, 2003).

facilitation of a renaissance of expository preaching and calling for evangelicals to facilitate more of the work of the Spirit within that context;[14] and Loader's helpful example in providing imaginative and exegetical readings of the New Testament.[15]

In arriving at a working definition of the imagination for the purposes of preaching, it is helpful to consider the contributions of two nineteenth-century figures: George MacDonald and Cardinal John Henry Newman. They offer helpful insights because in the Second Millennium and up until the nineteenth century, "imagination was treated as a dim-witted Cinderella to be kept in the poverty of her kitchen."[16] Nineteenth-century Romanticism was the "Fairy Godmother" for the restoration of the imagination, and such a shift in fortunes impacted theology.[17] MacDonald's and Newman's writings emerged in this period. MacDonald posits that the imagination is the way by which humanity can know God.[18] His understanding is that the imagination is not so much a human faculty with the power to create, as a divine gift by which to discover God. MacDonald advances the idea that creation is the form by which humanity can fill the world with thought, revelation and discoveries. "The man has but to light the lamp within the form [the world]: his imagination is the light, it is not the form. Straightway the shining thought makes the form visible, and becomes itself visible through the form."[19] In essence, there is nothing that humanity can claim as being of purely human origin; there is only the unearthing and discovering that which God has created and put in place. Although God is Creator, God opts to cooperate with humanity so that they may create:

> The glory of God is to conceal a thing, but the glory of the king is to find it out," says Solomon. "As if," remarks Bacon on the passage, "according to the innocent play of children, the Divine Majesty took delight to hide his works, to the end to have them

---

14. Greg Heisler, *Spirit-led Preaching: The Holy Spirit's Role in Sermon Preparation and Delivery* (Nashville: B & H, 2007).

15. William Loader, *The New Testament with Imagination: A Fresh Approach to Its Writings and Themes* (Grand Rapids: Eerdmans, 2007).

16. Gallagher, "Theology and Imagination," first paragraph.

17. Ibid.

18. George MacDonald, *A Dish of Orts* (Publishing details unknown, 1887).

19. Ibid., 5.

found out; and as if kings could not obtain a greater honour than to be God's playfellows in that game.[20]

To exercise the imagination is to become more human by becoming attuned to the purpose and presence of God. In his *Grammar of Assent*, written in 1892, Newman[21] suggests that the imagination has a place alongside reason to comprehend and embrace the reality of God. While he expresses a measure of concern about involving the imagination, he does not preclude its use as he states that reason alone cannot always be relied upon to advance good. Newman subsequently advances the idea that both reason and imagination are necessary for certitude of faith. He does tend to grant reason a slightly higher status, and he helpfully asserts the primacy of Scripture in it all, but the imagination is definitely a player in the venture of theology and faith. "I consider . . . that it is not reason that is against us, but imagination. The mind, after having, to the utter neglect of the Gospels, lived in science, experiences, on coming back to Scripture, an utter strangeness in what it reads."[22] Today, insofar as the gospel is concerned, the legacy is the same as Newman described: explanation of the gospel has overshadowed experience of the gospel.[23] The essence of Macdonald's and Newman's thesis is that the imagination attunes people to God and to his presence and activity in the world. They clarify its position by demonstrating its agency in comprehending God.

This book subscribes to such an understanding of the role and function of the imagination, especially when the imagination is actively engaging with Scripture and endeavouring to submit to the work of the Spirit. The imagination does not reveal *a* reality but *the* Reality. The imagination is the means by which God is discerned, experienced and comprehended, and by which life as directed by him is understood.[24] The imagination is not satisfied with the *status quo* but is the means by which God and his Word and love for this world can be taken seriously. Imaginative individuals and communities can begin to see the purposes of God for creation and are themselves

---

20. Ibid., 41.

21. John Henry Newman, *Grammar of Assent* (New York: Doubleday, 1955).

22. Quoted in Ellen F. Davis, *Imagination Shaped: Old Testament Preaching in the Anglican Tradition* (Valley Forge: Trinity Press, 1995), 249.

23. Peterson, *Under the Unpredictable Plant*.

24. William F. Lynch, *Images of Faith: An Exploration of the Ironic Imagination* (Notre Dame: Notre Dame Press, 1973); Cheryl Forbes, *Imagination: Embracing a Theology of Wonder* (Portland: Multnomah, 1986); Garret Green, *Imagining God: Theology and the Religious Imagination* (Grand Rapids: Eerdmans, 1989); Davis, *Imagination Shaped*.

harmoniously aligned with reality as ordered by God.[25] Brueggemann puts it masterfully when he writes of the "imaginative 'or'."[26] By drawing on Joshua and Isaiah, Brueggemann demonstrates how God presented a choice to his people. They could either continue to live without reference to God, *or* they could respond to and embrace the divine script for an alternative existence in keeping with salvation history.

However, it is often the case that the biblical witness is viewed as an appendage to current reality and is not considered seriously as reality in its own right. Peterson[27] considers this as evidence of the extent to which the imagination is atrophied. The Bible's description and vision of life and God's involvement in it is considered less than the world in which people live. For example, Peterson observes that people appeal for the Bible to be made relevant or to be accommodated into personal life routines, both well-intended pursuits but examples of the erroneous perception of seeing the "biblical world as smaller than the secular world."[28] The way to correct such an error is through the enlargement and formation of the imagination. The imagination in full force facilitates, if not demands, the presence of the whole person and not simply an emotional or cognitive presence. It draws on all the human faculties and calls forth action in response to that which is discerned and experienced through the imagination.[29] The most obvious and frequent example of this in the life of Christians today is communion. When the words of institution are uttered and the elements consumed, the imagination pictures the night when Christ was betrayed. The Christian responds with their will and finds faith and hope rising up, as they determine to be present to Christ and to love in new ways. Such use of the imagination bears out Newman's thesis that the imagination impacts the motivating forces in human life: forces such as hope, fear and passion. The imagination that is orientated towards God influences and stimulates these forces in accordance with his purpose.

What exacerbates the issue is that as a concept, the imagination suffers from a bad press. As a term, imagination is used interchangeably in complimentary

---

25. MacDonald, *A Dish of Orts*.

26. Walter Brueggemann, "An Imaginative 'Or,'" in *A Reader on Preaching: Making Connections*, ed. David Day, Jeff Astley and Leslie J. Francis (Aldershot: Ashgate, 2005), 51–64.

27. Eugene H. Peterson, *Eat This Book: A Conversation in the Art of Spiritual Reading* (Grand Rapids: Eerdmans, 2006).

28. Ibid., 67.

29. Lynch, *Images of Faith*; Green, *Imagining God*.

and derogatory ways. For instance, a leader can be complimented as being imaginative, while someone's contribution can be dismissed as being "just your imagination."[30] To suggest the use of the imagination within the context of Christian ministry, especially preaching, can cause unease. Troeger, with reference to preaching, states, "Imagination is not always a welcome guest in the household of faith."[31] This is probably because in common parlance, imagination is often associated with fantasy, day-dreaming and make-believe; imagination is confused with the imaginary.[32] Wiersbe makes a distinction between imagination and fancy (the imaginary). Imagination penetrates reality and aids understanding, while fancy endeavours to escape reality. "Fancy wrote 'Mary had a little lamb' but inspired imagination wrote 'The Lord is my Shepherd.' Fancy creates a new world for you; imagination gives you insight into the old world."[33]

Imagination might be more welcome, and the household of faith more at ease, if its relationship with Scripture was shown to be organic. The balance of the concern tends to be weighted towards the capacity of the imagination to generate constructions that are at best fanciful and at worst evil. Tozer comments that "the imagination, since it is a faculty of the natural mind, must necessarily suffer from its intrinsic limitations and from an inherent bent towards evil."[34] However, that possibility being stated, Tozer then warns of the loss if such fear is surrendered to. That loss is the inability to enjoy "the sacred gift of seeing, the ability to peer beyond the veil and gaze with astonished wonder upon the beauties and mysteries of things holy and eternal."[35]

MacDonald[36] also acknowledges the potential of the imagination to deceive and facilitate evil, but he responds by advocating the development of the imagination, not its suppression. In addition, MacDonald locates the origin of human imagination in the wisdom and light of God. So while the imagination may at times demonstrate evidence of being assaulted and shaped by sin, our hope rests in the fact that its genesis is not from darkness but from

---

30. Green, *Imagining God.*

31. Thomas H. Troeger, *Imaging a Sermon* (Nashville: Abingdon, 1990), 99.

32. Wiersbe, *Preaching and Teaching with Imagination.*

33. Wiersbe, quoted in Peterson, *Eat This Book*, 102.

34. A. W. Tozer, "The Value of a Sanctified Imagination," in *Developing a Christian Imagination: An Interpretive Anthology*, ed. Warren W. Wiersbe (Wheaton: Victor, 1995), 213.

35. Ibid., 213–214.

36. MacDonald, *A Dish of Orts.*

the goodness of God because, with specific reference to the imagination, "the Maker is our Light."[37] Insofar as the imagination represents the fallen human nature, it also represents a context for divine redemption. To suggest that the imagination is too dangerous and unreliable to be utilized is to suggest that there is an aspect of humanity which is beyond salvation – and that is patently not the case. "What the imagination does in its way . . . is to make a bold and difficult passage through darkness or fantasy or lies of all kinds, in order to build or discover a reality . . . In this, its first task, the imagination conquers fantasy."[38] An imagination shaped by Scripture and illuminated by the Spirit enables the scales to fall from our eyes so that reality as God has created it can be seen.

Against the backdrop of the struggle to faithfully study the Scriptures and apply them, to discern reality as ordained by God and to exercise an atrophied imagination, the preacher has a pivotal role. It falls to the preacher to model and mediate the use of the imagination in the pursuit of God. "To save sinners, God seizes them by the imagination: the preacher places himself at the service of this saving act by the obedient and lucid engagement of his own imagination."[39] Coupled with this is that the authors of the Scriptures, under the inspiration of the Spirit, had their imaginations quickened, and to plum the meaning of Scripture requires of "those who approach [Scripture] . . . an imagination as venturesome as the [writers of Scripture]."[40] The position of this research is that the focal point of salvation history and the event to which theological definitions of the imagination implicitly and explicitly lead is the incarnation. Insofar as the Christian view of the imagination is concerned, and especially for the purposes of preaching, the following working definition is therefore offered:

Imagination is the means of becoming attuned
to the ongoing reality
of the incarnation.

By its very nature, the incarnation displays the message of the Scripture, the immediacy of God, the innate dignity of humanity and the presence of the kingdom of God. The incarnation is light in the darkness, God's reality in

---

37. Ibid., 25.

38. William F. Lynch, *Images of Hope: Imagination as Healer of the Hopeless* (Notre Dame: Notre Dame Press, 1974), 244.

39. Green, *Imagining God*, 149.

40. Neil Gregor Smith, "Imagination in Exegesis," *Interpretation* 10, no. 4 (1956): 425.

the midst of pseudo-reality. "What imagination helps us see is that any life, no matter how ordinary, is extraordinary with God. He shattered ordinariness with the incarnation. We just haven't got the message yet."[41] Lloyd-Jones' catechistic question and answer sum up the case succinctly: "What is the chief end of preaching? To give men and women a sense of God and his presence."[42]

However, it is an irony that in the very study of the Scriptures the "systematic degradation of the imagination" can take place and those who study them "experience nothing . . . because the wonder has gone out of them." Attendant dangers are present when someone's profession involves the regular handling of the Scriptures. The spirit with which such a professional approaches the text can reduce it to the ordinary, and expediency can stifle attention. Merton observes that those professionally involved in the study of the Scriptures "can often manage to evade a radically involved dialogue with the book they are questioning"[43] and, in the process of intense concentration on isolated words and details, lose interest in their meaning. Merton comments further on the effects of becoming comfortable with the Bible to the extent that it no longer astonishes the reader. To preach the Scriptures requires the preacher to wrestle with the "disruptive givenness of the Bible"[44] and in turn to issue an invitation to the hearers to join the preacher in places where they have been led.[45] Schneiders identifies a suspicion "that slack-minded 'piety' is being substituted for serious study"[46] and so spirituality is separated from scholarship. Underlying this suspicion is the legacy of the Enlightenment, with "its obsession with the so-called objectivity of study, which seemed to require the disengagement of the researcher from any personal involvement with the subject matter being studied."[47] Thurston identifies the struggle between exegesis and the final form of a sermon, stating, "Historical-critical scholarship of the Bible immeasurably enriches preaching. But preaching is not historical-critical scholarship."[48] Schneiders issues a strong challenge in response to such an approach and makes the following observation:

---

41. Forbes, *Imagination*, 19.

42. Martyn Lloyd-Jones, *Preaching and Preachers* (London: Hodder & Stoughton, 1971), 97.

43. Thomas Merton, *Opening the Bible* (Collegeville: Liturgical Press, 1970), 34.

44. Gordon Oliver quoted in Bonnie Thurston, "On Biblical Preaching," *The Way* 48, no. 1 (2009): 75.

45. Thurston, "On Biblical Preaching."

46. Schneiders, "Biblical Spirituality," 141.

47. Ibid.

48. Thurston, "On Biblical Preaching," 78.

The resulting dichotomy in practice is deleterious for both biblical scholarship and spirituality. In reality the most intellectually rigorous and spiritually fruitful work on the biblical texts throughout history has been done by those who were not only speaking competently and even authoritatively to their academic peers but were also passionately concerned with spirituality: Origen, Augustine, Thomas Aquinas, Bonaventure, Bernard, Luther, Calvin, Bultmann, Barth, Lagrange, Raymond Brown, and many others.[49]

Serious scholarship and passionate spirituality are complements not combatants.

The Bible calls forth a response in the reader, and Bultmann suggested that this requires two levels of understanding.[50] The first level is the study of the text, while the second is a deeper and more personal engagement with it. The first level is preparation for the second level. However, the danger comes when what is understood through the first level, historical-critical study, is taken as the final meaning.[51] Raymond Brown signalled the limitations of exegetical study: "[W]hat is grasped through the historical-critical method is not the whole meaning of the Bible."[52] Burghardt's lament is apt: "The exegetes have taken away my Lord, and I know not where they have laid him."[53] The effect is not unlike the prophetic vision of Ezekiel, with dry bones needing to be animated by the breath of God (Ezek 37:1–14). To engage with the text solely at the first level is to run the risk of being left with a lifeless pile of bones. As von Balthasar put it, "contemporary exegesis has managed to reduce the living body of Scripture to an inert mess of blood and bones."[54] The first level must be allowed to do its work of setting the direction, "like a torchbeam

49. Schneiders, "Biblical Spirituality," 141.

50. Merton, *Opening the Bible.*

51. Ibid. Brendan Byrne, "'To See with the Eyes of the Imagination . . .': Scripture in the Exercises and Recent Interpretation," *The Way* 72 (1991): 3–19. It will be seen in chapter 4 that this research found it more beneficial to reverse the order of the two levels described by Merton when utilizing *lectio divina* and Ignatian Gospel Contemplation. Hence, exegetical work was engaged in *after* prayer and personal engagement with the text. Hereafter, references to the first level (exegesis of Scripture) and second level (personal engagement with the text) are used as descriptive categories rather than giving an indication of the sequence in which they were employed in this research.

52. Raymond Brown quoted in Thurston, "On Biblical Preaching," 78.

53. Burghardt, *Preaching: The Art and the Craft*, 8.

54. Von Balthasar quoted in Christopher Dillon, "Lectio Divina in the Monastic Tradition," *Cistercian Studies Quarterly* 34 (1999): 318.

which from a single point produces an ever widening but nonetheless directed beam of light."[55] It must be allowed to reveal "the 'otherness' of the biblical record, the 'distance' of the world it presupposes,"[56] guard against eisegesis and ensure a general coherence with the overall witness of Scripture and the church.[57] However, if this first level is granted sole status, the imagination of the preacher is suppressed and the resultant impression for hearers is that the Word of God "arrives in a hermetically sealed tube."[58] The second level, informed by the first, is the point at which the imagination is engaged:

> But powerful biblical preaching goes beyond critical scholarship. Indeed, it uses scholarship as a springboard into the mysteries of faith. Powerful biblical preaching comes from preachers who believe, and who have glimpsed the One whose shadow is seen in the text.[59]

To pay attention only while conducting exegesis does not go far enough: attention must also be focused at the second and more personal level. "The text should be known as it stands, in its intellectual-affective integrity. We need to let it resonate within us. We need to feel it so that we can know it connaturally."[60] The challenge is to possess what Paul Ricoeur described as a "second naïveté" in encountering the Scriptures.[61] The effect is a holistic engagement with the text and presentation of it through subsequent preaching.

Also, at both levels, Scripture needs to be approached on the understanding that its premise is that God invites, if not demands, a response from humanity:

> One of the basic truths put forward in the Bible as a whole is not merely that God is always right and man is always wrong, but that God and man can face each other in an authentic dialog: one which implies *a true reciprocity between persons, each of whom fully respects the other's rights and his freedom* . . . The whole idea of covenant, dialog, reciprocity, mutual respect . . . is brought out by giving the exchange a frankly human character. "Then the Lord said to Moses . . . Then Moses replied." To complain of this

---

55. Byrne, "Scripture in the Exercises," 14.

56. Ibid.

57. Ibid. Schneiders, "Biblical Spirituality."

58. Thomas H. Troeger, *Imaging a Sermon* (Nashville: Abingdon, 1990), 27.

59. Thurston, "On Biblical Preaching," 78.

60. Kenneth C. Russell, "Why Lectio Divina is Difficult," *Spiritual Life* 49 (2003): 73.

61. Thurston, "On Biblical Preaching," 67.

is not to give evidence of superior mystical wisdom, but only of literal-mindedness and weak imagination.[62]

Hence, all study of Scripture for the purpose of preaching demands personal surrender to its voice. "Any serious reading of the Bible means personal involvement in it, not simply mental agreement with abstract propositions. And involvement is dangerous, because it lays one open to unforeseen conclusions."[63] Such "involvement" facilitates the birth of a biblically formed recovery of the imagination for the purposes of Christian ministry. We are confronted with an overwhelming opportunity of discovery in approaching Scripture:

> There is an excess of meaning in God's word, whether it be the first word of Creation, the Eternal Word or the word of revelation. Our sharp logical categories are just not adequate. Nor our dualistic antinomies, a purely dialectic methodology of either/or. The reality is both/and: both life and death, eternity and history, myth and fact, revelation and reason, spiritual and empirical, unity and duality and even trinity, dialectic and analogy, stability and adaptability, truth and indeterminacy.[64]

In her discussion of "biblical spirituality," Schneiders offers several meanings of the term, one of which is "a transformative process of personal and communal engagement with the biblical text."[65] Schneiders complements Merton's call. With the minister especially in view, she affirms that the Bible must be approached not merely as a historical document but as the Word of God. Thurston describes the second level of understanding not so much as explaining as "inviting people to an unpredictable future encounter with the great Mystery of God. And that can be profoundly disruptive! But, again, the preacher can only invite others into what is his or her own experience."[66] Consequently, scholarship and spirituality need to be present in the study of the Scriptures:

---

62. Merton, *Opening the Bible*, 44–45, emphasis in original.

63. Ibid., 43.

64. Basil M. Pennington, *Who Do You Say I Am? Meditations on Jesus' Questions in the Gospels* (New York: New City Press, 2005), 18.

65. Schneiders, "Biblical Spirituality," 136.

66. Thurston, "On Biblical Preaching," 78.

Such an approach, rooted in faith, cannot bypass historical-critical exegesis and literary analysis. This is evident in the case of the biblical scholar whose role in the church is precisely to study the sacred text . . . [and] even the non-specialist who is serious about entering into relationship with God through this text must make the effort required to understand the text "on its own terms" . . . it requires willingness to be not only affirmed but also interrogated by that which is "other," by that which challenges us to fidelity in the living of our Christian vocation and strengthens us to do so in ways that can be genuinely surprising.[67]

Perhaps the dialogue between Jesus and Peter, when many disciples turned away because of the difficulty of his teaching, puts it best: "So Jesus asked the twelve, 'Do you also wish to go away?' Simon Peter answered him, 'Lord, to whom can we go? You have the words of eternal life'" (John 6:67–69).

How, then, can the imagination be employed so that it is synchronized with the first level of sound exegesis? How can the imagination be utilized so that the aforementioned fears and suspicions concerning imagination are not realized? How can the kind of involvement Merton calls for be facilitated? Wiersbe comments that while many books address exegetical and hermeneutical issues, "they fail to explain the important part the imagination plays in *pulling the whole thing together so that we can see what the writer is saying*."[68] Peterson explains the powerful contribution imagination plays in revealing the greater whole: "Imagination is the capacity to make connections between the visible and the invisible, between heaven and earth, between present and past, between present and future."[69] Peterson extends the thesis that imagination and explanation need to work together:

Explanation pins things down so that we can handle and use them – obey and teach, help and guide. Imagination opens things up so that we can grow into maturity – worship and adore, exclaim and honor, follow and trust . . . Explanation reduces life to what can be used; Imagination enlarges life into what can be adored.[70]

---

67. Schneiders, "Biblical Spirituality," 136.

68. Wiersbe, *Preaching and Teaching with Imagination*, 28–29, emphasis in original.

69. Peterson, *Under the Unpredictable Plant*, 169.

70. Ibid., 171–172.

He goes on to observe that "in the life of the gospel . . . Imagination and Explanation cannot get along without each other."[71] Troeger succinctly summarizes the challenge and provides a helpful response: "What, then, are the principles for using our imaginations so that we can receive the *ruach*, the Spirit of the living God to whom our preaching is a witness? The primary principle from which all the others are derived is that we are attentive to what is."[72]

A way to facilitate the necessary organic relationship between exegetical study and imagination, between the first and second levels of reading Scripture, between Explanation and Imagination, is through *praying* the Scriptures. Perhaps Burghardt puts it best:

> Still, Luther was on target: Scholarly tomes and commentaries are "no more than a tool with which to build aright, so that we can understand, taste and abide in the simple and pure word of God." The word we study calls for *contemplation*: It "must be contemplated with a quiet mind." The Bible is not Blackstone's *Commentaries* or Einstein's theory of relativity; it is a book to be prayed.[73]

So an approach in prayer which enables the Bible to be prayed in an exegetically accurate and imaginative way is required. This research proposes two forms of prayer which embrace and respond to the aforementioned issues: *lectio divina* and Ignatian Gospel Contemplation.

Writing about *lectio divina* in the twelfth century, William of St Thierry provided a vision of how the organic relationship between sound exegetical work and the application of the imagination in the reading and praying of Scripture can be embraced. He exhorts that the various genres of Scripture must be read in the same spirit in which they were written:

> You will never reach an understanding of Paul until, by close attention to reading him and the application of continual reflection, you imbibe his spirit. You will never arrive at understanding David until by actual experience you realize what the psalms are about. And so it is with the rest. In every piece of Scripture, real attention is as different from mere reading as

71. Ibid., 172.
72. Troeger, *Imaging a Sermon*, 15.
73. Burghardt, *Preaching: The Art and the Craft*, 86–87, emphasis in original.

friendship is from entertainment, or the love of a friend from a casual greeting.[74]

The implication of William of St Thierry's call and the tradition he represents is to "develop an affinity of mind with [the Scriptures] and consciously avoid all that deadens our awareness of reality . . . If we start by trusting our imagination, we must go on to trust that to which, in images and metaphors, it leads us."[75] This requires trust that the first level of understanding is reached but that it is not the final meaning: the imagination now so empowered must be allowed to do its work prayerfully. *Lectio divina* and Ignatian Gospel Contemplation rest on immersion in the Scripture at hand and draw on the imagination. While the forms of prayer were especially developed in the Middle Ages (*lectio divina* in the twelfth century) and Early Modern Period (Ignatian Gospel Contemplation in the sixteenth century), their emergence, development and use in the preceding centuries and their use subsequent to the twelfth and sixteenth centuries demonstrate an extraordinary enduring relevance and applicability to all epochs. They especially present an applicable response to contemporary issues in preaching. For instance, in the twelfth century, *lectio divina* gained traction in a time marked by "the sad effect of a spirituality isolated from theological reflection and of a theology deprived of mystery."[76] Such a description is disturbingly accurate of features of contemporary Western Christianity and, specifically, preaching. In turn, Ignatian Contemplation offers a tantalizing prospect for preachers today. Brackley describes Ignatius of Loyola's approach as revolutionary: while "a child of his times, he also transcended them. He even transcends our own."[77] In 1966, Karl Rahner wrote that Ignatian spirituality "is not typical of our time; it is not characteristic of the modern era which is nearing its end. It is, rather, a sign of the approaching future."[78] This research experienced glimpses of the future Rahner predicted; these findings are described in chapter 4.

In a later publication, Rahner spoke further about the future when he wrote, "The Christian of the future will be a mystic or he will not exist at

---

74. William of St Thierry quoted in Squire, *Asking the Fathers*, 124.

75. Squire, *Asking the Fathers*, 126.

76. Keith J. Egan, "Guigo II: The Theology of the Contemplative Life," in *The Spirituality of Western Christendom*, ed. E. Rozanne Elder (Kalamazoo, MI: Cistercian, 1976), 109.

77. Dean Brackley, *The Call to Discernment in Troubled Times: New Perspectives on the Transformative Wisdom of Ignatius of Loyola* (New York: Crossroad, 2004), 6.

78. Karl Rahner quoted in Brackley, *Call to Discernment*, 6.

all."[79] Endean helpfully paraphrases Rahner's admonition in order to expose
the theology behind it: "Tomorrow's devout person will either be a mystic
– someone who has 'experienced' something – or else they will no longer
be devout at all."[80] Endean explains that the "experience" will be grace
which will have its outworkings in the world. The use of *lectio divina* and
Ignatian Gospel Contemplation, and their ability to facilitate an integrated
relationship between exegetical work and the imagination, provide the means
for the kind of mysticism and experience Rahner describes. They hold the
promise to reintroduce into humanity the lost experience and wonder that
D. H. Lawrence[81] lamented and to aid the recovery of the imagination that
Peterson[82] calls for.

Elsewhere, Rahner discusses the tension between a systematic and
conceptual knowledge of God and a "primal relationship"[83] with God. His
description sets the context which precedes study and the necessary "radically
involved dialogue" with Scripture,[84] and the Divine Presence before which
the first and second levels of understanding of Scripture take place. He writes,
"Be still for once. Don't try to think of so many complex and varied things.
Give those deeper realities of the spirit a chance now to rise to the surface:
silence, fear, the ineffable longing for truth, for love, for fellowship, for God."[85]
Rahner is essentially serving a reminder of the primacy of God *before* any
theological work, prayer or meditation; "We love because he first loved
us" (1 John 4:19). Rahner is articulating the context in which all study and
engagement with the Scriptures takes place: in the presence of a transcendent
and immanent God. Without such an appreciation and experience, Rahner
contends, the result is a lack of credibility in the attempt to connect with
contemporary society in the name of God, including through the agency of
preaching. "Whenever piety is directed only by an ingenious, complicated
intellectuality and conceptuality, with highly complicated theological tenets,

---

79. Karl Rahner, *The Spirituality of the Church of the Future* (Publishing details unknown,
1981), 149.

80. Philip Endean, *Karl Rahner and Ignatian Spirituality* (Oxford: Oxford University Press,
2001), 63.

81. Squire, *Asking the Fathers.*

82. Peterson, *Under the Unpredictable Plant.*

83. Karl Rahner, *The Practice of Faith* (New York: Crossroad, 1986), 63.

84. Merton, *Opening the Bible*, 34.

85. Rahner, *The Practice of Faith*, 63.

it is really a pseudo-piety, however profound it may seem."[86] The two ancient forms of prayer, *lectio divina* and Ignatian Gospel Contemplation, facilitate and honour the space which Rahner describes and hopes for.

Complementary to Rahner's thought is the observation by Goldingay[87] that the post-modern era affords an opportunity to revisit the way Scripture is interpreted. In surveying the features of pre-modern, modern and post-modern biblical interpretation, Goldingay describes not only the landscape of current biblical scholarship but also the spiritual practice of Christians in applying Scripture to day-to-day life. Each era has its own nuances and limitations in the treatment of Scripture:

> Pre-modernity and modernity make two quite different assumptions about the way a text comes to speak to people . . . Pre-modernity assumed that the royal road to good interpretation was the assumption that the text spoke to our current concerns. It then found that it did so, though it was limited to seeing what spoke to its existent concerns and its nature did not allow for these to be broadened out so that they matched the text's concerns. Modernity assumed that the royal road to good interpretation was the setting aside of our concerns in order to focus on the text's, but there were problems with its practice . . . The text was concerned to feed a community's self-understanding by reminding it of God's involvement with it, but modernity was preoccupied with questions about history that it naively treated as if they were also the text's preoccupation. It never reached the text's agenda.[88]

Goldingay comments further that, even so, pre-modern interpretation is still predominant in the church. An apparent snatch-and-grab approach to texts is evident in an array of Christian settings, from ecumenical documents, preaching and personal guidance. The current post-modern era offers an opportunity to take the best of the pre-modern, modern and post-modern interpretative approaches and provide a working solution to the challenges articulated by the aforementioned writers. The post-moderns' commitment to the narrative genre, coupled with the strength of modern interpretation

---

86. Ibid.

87. John Goldingay, *An Ignatian Approach to Reading the Old Testament* (Cambridge: Grove, 2002).

88. Goldingay, "Premodern, Modern, and Postmodern," 19.

in creating necessary distance from the text to retain its integrity, and the immediacy of pre-modern interpretation with its confidence that God speaks directly through the text (at times regardless of its historical context) sets up a tantalizing opportunity. "The pre-Reformation Christian traditions, and especially the Eastern Churches, have never lost sight of the 'life force' of Scripture, and perhaps this is the direction in which post-Reformation churches must now grow."[89] Ramsey distils such issues down to a simple and obvious point and in doing so adds to the understanding of the opportunity today:

> We, sons and daughters of a more rational age, are not readily comfortable with the logic of Fathers, a logic that does not progress: major, minor and conclusion, one point after another. Rather one thought, one image, the color of one word leads off to another . . . But isn't this the way it usually happens when we are sitting with a friend in conversation? One idea leads to another, one thought gives birth to another, image after image evokes memories and facts. We don't usually worry too much about the logical sequence of our conversation and sharing. But it is so satisfying because it doesn't stay in the head, it calls forth imagination, memory and emotion, and lodges in the heart.[90]

Into this current era, *lectio divina* and Ignatian Contemplation present themselves as veterans providing the means for Christians to interpret the biblical text throughout the ages and hear the voice of God. They honour the primacy of God; they honour the two levels of understanding when studying and reading Scripture; and they advance the godly use of the imagination as a result.

The challenges faced by *lectio divina* and Ignatian Gospel Contemplation are not entirely dissimilar from the issues previously discussed in engaging with Scripture beyond the first level of understanding. A salutary fact to bear in mind is that the architect of the *lectio divina* schema, Guido II, lived during the advent of scholasticism in the twelfth century. His development of *lectio divina* was an acknowledgement of the new reverence for reason and yet also respect for the heritage of *lectio divina* from the Patristic era.[91] Consequently,

---

89. Thurston, "On Biblical Preaching," 74.

90. Pennington, *Who Do You Say I Am?*, 18.

91. Egan, "Guigo II"; Russell, "Why Lectio Divina is Difficult."

the elements of *lectio divina* have a rational flavour and yet also facilitate the spiritual:

> In his definition of *lectio* Guido speaks of the very careful investigation of the Scriptures through the attention of the mind . . . He sees *meditatio* as the studious action of the mind, investigating the knowledge of hidden truth under the impetus of one's reason . . . *Oratio* is defined in terms of the heart and *contemplatio* in terms of the traditional monastic imagery of taste, but through the elevation of the mind in suspension to God.[92]

Guido utilized allegory in a restrained fashion and was not comfortable with leaving interpretation of the biblical text at the merely literal, historical and rational level. Insofar as this was the case, Guido's contribution formulated an approach which accommodates the various emphases of historical interpretative priorities both then (twelfth century) and now. His schema did not demarcate between study and *lectio divina*, but from the thirteenth century onwards, as the influence of scholasticism and the Renaissance and Enlightenment eras took hold, until today, such a wedge was driven between the two:

> We certainly acknowledge that we need more than a merely scholarly insight into the text, its time, and its human author, but this more personal, "felt" aspect is regarded as a secondary, derivative benefit. The intellectual and the spiritual must each take its position at different levels of our being . . . This erroneous approach to Scripture [splitting the intellectual and spiritual] . . . is hard to correct because the historical-critical method has been the gatekeeper of Scripture's truth for some time now.[93]

The legacy of the Enlightenment still casts a shadow over contemporary study of the text and the nuances of meanings, and even the dominance of metaphor in Scripture fails to be recognized. "Reading scripture on different levels of meaning breaks open the historical-critical stranglehold and allows for creative and faithfully meaningful readings."[94] However, a recovery of *lectio divina* in its purest form has the potential to rejuvenate a ministry of

---

92. Egan, "Guigo II," 111–112.

93. Russell, "Why Lectio Divina is Difficult," 71.

94. Kathryn Green-McCreight quoted in Thurston, "On Biblical Preaching," 70.

preaching empowered by the imagination and based on "scholarly insight," thereby relaxing the "historical-critical stranglehold" and facilitating "creative and faithfully meaningful readings."

Similarly, Ignatius of Loyola developed an established form of prayer and adapted it not just for his time (sixteenth century) but as a timeless approach to the Scriptures gifted to the church. While in the Patristic period there was little effort or call to employ the imagination in engaging with the life of Christ as recorded in the Gospels, by the eleventh and twelfth centuries this had changed significantly:[95]

> How is it that in the West, toward the eleventh and twelfth centuries, all that changes? First the limits of the pathetic [feelings/emotions] are broadened, then those of the imagination . . . Read St Augustine, St Leo, St Gregory on the Nativity or the Passion, and then go on to St Bernard, William of St Thierry, St Bonaventure, and you will feel the difference. Just as the contemplation of the first named is hieratic, doctrinal, taken up especially with the divine life, or with the mystical body of Christ in us, so the latter are concerned with the man in Jesus, the man like us, and it is this thought that moves them.

From the thirteenth century, and during the next three to four centuries especially, the use of the imagination in engaging with the Scriptures gained traction. This resulted in some fanciful and far-fetched results. Ignatius' work was a corrective and he sought to establish a "true historical foundation"[96] while drawing on the best of the tradition. In essence, Ignatius simplified and clarified the tradition and introduced a needful pragmatism to it.[97] "For he [Ignatius] is more precise than the older writers of the twelfth century, and infinitely simpler than the writers of the fifteenth."[98] Significantly, Ignatius' work was during the height of the Reformation and Counter-Reformation, and all that represented and entailed concerning the treatment of Scripture. Thus, both Guido and Ignatius established prayerful approaches to the study of and engagement with Scripture during periods of significant historical and ecclesiastical change. Their contributions and approaches to Scripture

---

95. Alexandre Brou, *Ignatian Methods of Prayer* (Milwaukee: Bruce, 1949), 133.

96. Ibid., 137.

97. Joseph de Guibert, *The Jesuits: Their Spiritual Doctrine and Practice – A Historical Study* (Chicago: Institute of Jesuit Sources, 1964).

98. Brou, *Ignatian Methods of Prayer*, 11.

resonated with the culture of the day and yet were not restrained by it. *Lectio divina* and Ignatian Gospel Contemplation retain the integrity of Scripture and the life of the Spirit in whatever age these forms of prayer are being exercised. Thurston writes, "In biblical preaching we begin to throw off the chains that bind us primarily by entering the story ourselves, by becoming active participants and not observers in God's salvation history . . . This story continues in us, and in those to whom we proclaim it, or it does not continue at all."[99] *Lectio divina* and Ignatian Gospel Contemplation facilitate the living story with reverence, dynamism and Spirit-inspired imagination.

Today's preachers live in an exhilarating time. The opportunity to utilize the best of historical-critical study continues along with the challenge to enrich that by rediscovering the power of the imagination. This chapter has surveyed the wisdom of theologians and spiritual leaders over the centuries regarding how to integrate exegetical study and imaginative engagement with the text. We have seen that, more recently, theologians and writers have revived the call to engage the imagination with preaching. They have asserted that exegesis and imagination belong together and that one without the other is lacking, with the people of God poorer as a result. This exposé of the problem and the provision of a prophetic solution is compelling. *Lectio divina* and Ignatian Gospel Contemplation stand as agents which together act as a catalyst for sound exegesis and Spirit-inspired imaginative involvement with Scripture. Their genius rests on their insistence on the primacy of Scripture and their dependence on the Spirit to form the imagination. While both prayer disciplines are centuries old, they have retained a timelessness that enables them to provide a way forward for preachers today. Their ancient origins and contemporary relevance might appear paradoxical. However, as we now turn our attention to their form in their original setting and their applicability today, we will see their profound contribution for today's church.

---

99. Thurston, "On Biblical Preaching," 80.

2

Lectio Divina and Ignatian Gospel Contemplation: Then and Now

The new practitioner of *lectio divina* and Ignatian Gospel Contemplation is akin to the three disciples ascending the Mount of Transfiguration (Mark 9:2–8) or the two on the road to Emmaus (Luke 24:13–35). What starts out as relatively ordinary and familiar can sometimes become overwhelming, beyond comprehension and utterly revelatory. The outcome of such an encounter can mean further wrestling with the mystery of Christ (Mark 9:9–13) or immediate action in making known the news about the resurrected Christ (Luke 24:33–35). To help accommodate such potential outcomes of these two agencies of prayer, attention to key issues surrounding *lectio divina* and Ignatian Gospel Contemplation is required. Such issues include an appreciation of the genesis of both prayers, of their fluidity and rhythms, and of how Scripture is read when praying in these ways, and a clarification of the prayers' elements. Attention will be given first to *lectio divina* and then to Ignatian Gospel Contemplation.

Lectio Divina

For those unacquainted with *lectio divina*, its presentation can be deceptively simplistic. It appears to be little more than four simple steps:
- *Lectio* (reading) – reading the text aloud
- *Meditatio* (meditation) – ruminating on the text
- *Oratio* (prayer) – praying in response to the text
- *Contemplatio* (contemplation) – dwelling with the text

As mentioned in chapter 1, the author of this schema was Guido II, the ninth prior of the Grande Chartreuse in France. While *lectio divina* had been in use for a thousand years preceding him, Guido was the first to capture it in the form we know today.[1] Guido wrote *Scala Claustralium* (*The Ladder of the Monks*), and while he described the elements of *lectio divina* as four rungs of a ladder, it was not his intention that it should be a mechanical process. His writings were a reflection of his time, and the best application of his work is by St John of the Cross, who, referring to the four rungs, wrote, "Seek in reading and you will find in meditation; knock in prayer and it will be opened to you in contemplation."[2] St John of the Cross' words embody Guido's intent that *lectio divina* is both causal and integrated. The interplay in his schema between reason and heart, sequence and integration, is seen in Guido's own commentary on *lectio divina*:

> From what has been said we may gather that reading without meditation is dry. Meditation without reading is subject to error. Prayer without meditation is lukewarm. Meditation without prayer is fruitless. Prayer with devotion leads to contemplation whereas contemplation without prayer happens rarely or by a miracle.[3]

The relaxation into integration when reading the Bible instead of the creation of a dichotomy between head and heart is important. "If we read the Bible and other texts that unite thought and feeling as we should read any work of literature – slowly and reflectively – we will be doing *lectio divina*. There will be nothing artificial about it . . . There will be no need, first, to study and then to read spiritually."[4] *Lectio divina* facilitates dialogue and relationship with God which is dynamic rather than formulaic.

To engage with *lectio divina* in a mechanical way is to unwittingly domesticate it and reduce an encounter with God to a method. "*Lectio* is a disciplined form of devotion and not a method of Bible study. It is done

---

1. Egan, "Guigo II"; Russell, "Why Lectio Divina is Difficult."

2. St John of the Cross, quoted in Egan, "Guigo II," 108.

3. Quoted in Casey, *Sacred Reading*, 62.

4. Russell, "Why Lectio Divina is Difficult," 75.

purely and simply to come and to know God, to be brought before His Word, to listen."[5] Peterson issues a similar warning:

> *Lectio divina* is not a methodical technique for reading the Bible. It is a cultivated, developed habit of *living* the text in Jesus' name. This is the way, the *only* way, that the Holy Scriptures become formative in the Christian church and become salt and leaven in the world.[6]

While the student of *lectio divina* may need to begin their learning of *lectio divina* by carefully attending to each element in turn, this needs to be imbued with an understanding and expectation that God is active and present.[7] Yet to discern and experience God can often mean wrestling with his apparent absence and silence. *Lectio divina* provides the reader with the opportunity and means to struggle and search for God. We approach *lectio divina* with a desire for God and discover that "seeking may be more truthful than finding" and that "patient receptivity may serve us better than a clamorous urgency to be enlightened."[8] Thus, a mechanical, crisp and sequential approach to *lectio divina*, to listening to and speaking with God, would be to misappropriate this way of availing oneself for the work of the Spirit. The true spirit of *lectio divina* is one of fluidity and integration.

To appreciate the essential nature of *lectio divina*, the stages of *lectio divina* can be viewed as strands of the same cord or "different attitudes of the same gesture."[9] It has been variously described as a folk dance, a looping spiral, dangerous chemical elements combining to create a helpful compound,[10] or movements which ebb and flow, join and separate.[11] Moreover, *lectio divina* is a lifestyle rather than a method. "*Lectio divina* is a way of life that develops 'according to the Scriptures'. It is not just a skill that we exercise when we have a Bible open before us but a life congruent with the Word made flesh to which the Scriptures give witness."[12] Guido considered the four rungs of the

---

5. Gabriel O'Donnell, "Reading for Holiness: Lectio Divina," in *Spiritual Traditions for the Contemporary Church*, ed. Robin Maas and Gabriel O'Donnell (Nashville: Abingdon, 1990), 47.

6. Peterson, *Eat This Book*, 116, emphasis in original.

7. Mary C. Earle, "The Process of Lectio Divina," *The Lutheran* 16 (2003).

8. Casey, *Sacred Reading*, 8.

9. Ernest J. Fiedler, "Lectio Divina: Devouring God's Word," *Liturgical Ministry* 5 (1996): 68.

10. Peterson, *Eat This Book*, 91.

11. Casey, *Sacred Reading*.

12. Peterson, *Eat This Book*, 318.

lectio divina ladder as collapsing into each other. He viewed *lectio* as being prolonged by *meditatio*, which became *oratio* in and of itself; and these three elements conspired to become *contemplatio*.[13] The result was not an exercise in piety but a life being formed: "In the actual practice of *lectio divina* the four elements fuse, interpenetrate. *Lectio divina* is a way of reading that becomes a way of living."[14] It violates the spirit of *lectio divina* to term it as a method per se. In this book we will employ the terms "discipline" and "practice" instead.

One helpful way to view *lectio divina* is also probably the oldest: gastronomically. This was a common monastic way of explaining the means to approach the Scriptures and their spiritual effect, drawing on the exhortation to "taste and see that the LORD is good" (Ps 34:8). With the bread and wine of the Lord's Supper especially in mind, Scriptures were likewise "consumed" for a similar effect:

> . . . there is a litany of nouns and verbs to be found: "taste," "nourish," "consume," "food," "ruminate," "digest," "savor," "palate," "cud" . . . and even a term that some cultures view as crude, "belch." Early Christian writers have considered all of these words helpful in teaching us to learn to pray Scripture intimately, thus finding God's word essential food for our spiritual life and growth.[15]

The connection between the literal tasting of the bread and wine and the reading of the Scriptures was that such nourishment leads to Christlikeness. Specifically, Guido applied gastronomic functions to each of the four elements of *lectio divina*. *Lectio* is the solid food; *meditatio* chews and breaks it up; *oratio* savours it; and *contemplatio* enjoys its sustenance.[16] The result is craving for more of this divine food. Indeed, the practice of *lectio divina* not only has nutritional value; such food also has medicinal effect. *Lectio divina* can address the dying soul which no longer feeds itself and bears the burdens and afflictions of life. For the one experiencing the "piety void,"[17] with all its attendant guilt-issues, *lectio divina* is a tonic: one of the most effective ways back after a drought of the Word.

---

13. Fiedler, "Lectio Divina."
14. Ibid., 68.
15. Ibid., 67.
16. Egan, "Guigo II."
17. Casey, *Sacred Reading*, 31.

Lectio

The step we call *lectio* should begin with prayer. Then a passage of Scripture is chosen as the focus of *lectio divina*. A short passage of Scripture is preferred as the entire process is to be constantly interspersed with and interrupted by prayer.[18] Prayer is the language; the four moments of *lectio divina* are merely variations of the themes and topics of the prayer conversation taking place:

> Fundamentally it is the atmosphere of prayer that penetrates every aspect of holy reading that makes it distinctive. Prayer is not suddenly born at the third stage [*oratio*]. Rather, prayer accompanies us as we open the book and settle our mind, as we read the page and ponder its meaning. Prayer is the meaning of *lectio divina*; that is why the exercise of sacred reading is sometimes said to be a technique of prayer.[19]

What a musical instrument is to sheet music, so prayer is to *lectio divina*. To divorce any stage of *lectio divina* from prayer is like reading music without actually playing a musical instrument in response. At the very least, as the four movements of *lectio divina* are engaged with, a person ought to prayerfully hum along with the music it offers.

Once the text is selected, the person begins by reading aloud in a slow and careful manner just as one might read poetry. The intent is to listen for a particular word or phrase which captures the attention. This may happen in the first sentence read or only after repeated readings. "How far along we get in the text is less important than how open we are to the power and message if the text is leading us to authentic communication with God."[20] *Lectio divina* depends on a leisurely, careful and attentive reading pace. Such a style of reading may seem counter-intuitive and difficult in the presence of the busyness and pressures of pastoral ministry. Therefore, an appreciation of how Scripture was read through the agency of *lectio divina* centuries ago is salutary.

---

18. Adalbert de Vogue, *The Rule of Saint Benedict: A Doctrinal and Spiritual Commentary* (Kalamazoo: Cistercian, 1983); Fiedler, "Lectio Divina."

19. Casey, *Sacred Reading*, 61.

20. O'Donnell, "Reading for Holiness," 48.

When *lectio divina* was employed in ancient times, people did not read as we do now, silently and mentally.[21] The text was read aloud and, therefore, heard. "One reads, in the ancient sense of that word, with one's mouth and one's ears,"[22] and in antiquity reading rested on the sense that the text was primarily proclaimed and heard rather than seen. "*Lectio divina* was the art of listening."[23] A paradigm shift is required, then, to acknowledge that language is primarily to be heard rather than seen. The written word is "frozen speech,"[24] yet while the letter kills, the Spirit gives life (2 Cor 3:6). "We must remember that the Bible (which we think of as a book to be *read*) was originally a body of oral traditions meant to be *recited and listened to in a group especially attuned to its message*."[25] Lectio divina is one means by which the Spirit breathes life into the "letter" in concert with the human voice giving it warmth.[26]

"*Lectio* is listening to a Person present."[27] In the practice of reading the text aloud, the reader literally becomes the proclaimer and hearer of the Word of God.[28] The biblical interplay between *ruach* (spirit/breath) and *dabar* (word/deed), which begins in Genesis 1 and is demonstrated wonderfully in Ezekiel's vision (Ezek 37:4–14), is present in the moment of the reading, verbalizing and receiving the Word of God. This does not disqualify the need for exegesis or remembering that the Word of God was not written in English. Yet to read aloud must, at some level, revive the experience and intimacy of the relationship between *ruach* and *dabar*:

> For the Israelites, then, breath, the basis of "word," the sound made in inter-personal contact, had a dynamic quality that both communicated and brought about activity and being. The spoken word [*dabar*] which relied upon *ruach* was the means of this communication. *Dabar* was also an activity that had influential communicative and dynamic qualities. In summary,

---

21. O'Donnell, "Reading for Holiness"; Fiedler, "Lectio Divina"; Basil M. Pennington, *Lectio Divina: Renewing the Ancient Practice of Praying the Scriptures* (New York: Crossroad, 1998); Elizabeth Canham, *Praying the Bible*, 2nd ed. (Cincinnati: Forward Movement, 2001); Russell, "Why Lectio Divina is Difficult."

22. O'Donnell, "Reading for Holiness," 46.

23. Vincent Dwyer, "Many Paths to Prayer: Lectio Divina," accessed January 2015 at http://www.jesuits.ca/orientations/dwyer.html#transcription.

24. Russell, "Why Lectio Divina is Difficult," 67.

25. Merton, *Opening the Bible*, 53–54, emphasis in original.

26. Russell, "Why Lectio Divina is Difficult."

27. Pennington, *Lectio Divina*, 4.

28. O'Donnell, "Reading for Holiness."

every *dabar* was a "word-deed" . . . This biblical background to *ruach* and *dabar* is the foundation for our appreciation of the "Word of God" which we celebrate and proclaim in our liturgies. The Word of God addresses the baptized community of Jesus' sisters and brothers. The Word effects; it has the power to impact, change, enliven and consolidate.[29]

Hence, the simple discipline of reading Scripture aloud reminds the reader that the Word of God is not paper and ink but the Divine at work in the world of flesh and blood. Thus *lectio divina* facilitates the promise of Christ which is especially evident in John 8:31; 14:23; and 15:7: the interrelatedness of abiding in the Word and God abiding with the disciple.[30] So this first element of *lectio divina* is not simply acquainting oneself with the text at hand. Through the agency of the human voice and hearing, the voice of God begins to take effect. The Word is received by literally hearing, and the disciple is prepared for *meditatio*.

Meditatio

Meditatio is the element of *lectio divina* when the arresting word or phrase which emerged during *lectio* is embraced. As will be discussed below, *meditatio* can be conducted with Bible in hand or as a person goes about their daily activity. Either way can bear much fruit:

> At this stage your interest is in the present: where is this text happening – "being fulfilled" – in your life and world? You find the answer to this question in a natural spontaneous way. Either: something in the text reminds you of something in your experience. Or: something in your experience reminds you of the text.[31]

The key to *meditatio* is to actively ponder, wonder at and wrestle with the word or phrase using questions such as: "Why of all the words read has this particular one caught my imagination?"; "What is the appeal, challenge, dissonance or comfort of this word?"; or even "How does this make me

---

29. Michael Trainor, "Towards a Parish Spirituality of the Word of God," *Compass* 42, no. 4 (2008): no page number.

30. O'Donnell, "Reading for Holiness"; Fiedler, "Lectio Divina"; Dillon, "Lectio Divina."

31. Michel de Verteuil, "Lectio Divina," Dominican Biblical Institute, accessed 3 June 2009 at http://www.dbclimerick.ie/lectiodivina.php.

feel?" *Meditatio* provides the opportunity for serious reading and response to the text. In addition to the aforementioned questions, it may be helpful to consider various contexts to which the meaning of the text may apply. De Verteuil describes five levels at which a text might be fulfilled: between God and an individual, between people, within a person, between a community and a wider community, and within creation. This template is especially helpful given that this research has in view the creation of a sermon emerging from *lectio divina*. A preacher's utilization of the five levels would sharpen the focus of the meditation with a congregation in mind and God's message to them.

However, the simple, albeit correct, translation of the word *meditatio* as "meditation" can raise concerns for people unfamiliar with the term. An association is made with non-Christian meditative practices and the call for meditation here seems at odds with Christian discipleship. However, in the first millennium of church history, meditation meant holding a received word from *lectio* or a spiritual leader and nurturing it.[32] This was not solely a mental exercise but one which was allowed to permeate one's emotions and whole being. So in this stage of *lectio divina*, "Ideally, we would find a quiet corner and begin actually to 'mumble' the text . . . While mumbling the phrase we would 'ruminate' on it – ponder it, rest in it,"[33] or take that Word wherever we go.[34] In the tradition and counsel of St Benedict this would involve continuing *meditatio* as the daily routine, work and responsibilities are attended to.[35] The monastic modus operandi was *ora, labora, lege* (pray, work, read). In applying this to the rhythm of *lectio divina* for us today, we may find it fruitful to embrace *ora, labora, lege, meditare* (meditation).[36] As with *lectio*, *meditatio* is not necessarily a silent and interior exercise. It can involve the verbalizing of the text.[37] The intent is to be formed and changed by the Word. Meditation, in this sense, is not an exercise in transcendence but in incarnation. "*Lectio divina* is an expression of my search for God: Sacred reading can be considered 'successful' only if it causes me to drop my defences

---

32. Pennington, *Lectio Divina*.
33. O'Donnell, "Reading for Holiness," 47.
34. Pennington, *Lectio Divina*.
35. De Vogue, *The Rule of Saint Benedict*; Canham, *Praying the Bible*.
36. De Vogue, *The Rule of Saint Benedict*.
37. Ibid.

and allow God to touch my heart and change my life."[38] Hence, within the context of this research, the first person impacted will be the preacher.

A practical consideration is especially prominent at this stage of *lectio divina*: the presence of distractions. Such distractions can come in any number of ways: noise (external and internal), memories, daydreaming, tiredness, haste and so on. In the presence of such expected obstacles the counsel is to "*go back to the Word*, read on a bit further. Use the Word of God as your safeguard, your guide. Don't fight the devil; don't fight yourself. That is God's business."[39] Also, "There is no meditation without distraction. Return, then, to the reading. Concentrate on the key words."[40] As before, the verbalizing of the word or phrase can also enhance focus, attention, concentration and awareness of the work and presence of God as *lectio divina* unfolds.[41] The universal experience of distractions in prayer gave rise to the need for a defined approach in prayer and Guido's schema was, at least in some measure, a response to that.[42] As early as the fifth century, John Cassian powerfully described the problem of distractions in prayer and sought something which would "curb the restlessness of those feelings which come and go, and . . . master them."[43] Cassian further writes: "If we slip into this confusion it is clearly because we do not have something fixed before our eyes, something like a formula to which our wandering thoughts can be recalled from their wayfaring, a kind of harbor where they can find rest after the fury of the storm."[44] So *lectio divina* and Ignatian Gospel Contemplation are in and of themselves a foil to distractions present in less structured forms of contemplative prayer.

Just as true *lectio* depends on giving attention to sections of Scripture in context, so "Meditation is the aspect of spiritual reading that trains us to read Scripture as a connected, coherent whole, not a collection of inspired bits and pieces."[45] The word or phrase which has arrested the attention during *lectio* is ruminated over, questioned, pondered, repeated, explored and examined.

---

38. Casey, *Sacred Reading*, 62.

39. O'Donnell, "Reading for Holiness," 47, emphasis in original.

40. Fr Bernado Olivera quoted in Pennington, *Lectio Divina*, 160.

41. Fiedler, "Lectio Divina."

42. Brou, *Ignatian Methods of Prayer*.

43. John Cassian quoted in Brou, *Ignatian Methods of Prayer*, 2.

44. Ibid.

45. Peterson, *Eat This Book*, 101.

The imagination will come into play as it is guided and formed by the text.[46] "Meditation is the prayerful employ of imagination in order to become friends with the text."[47] However, *meditatio* is not a time of inventing fanciful and fictitious thoughts and visions, but the time when the weight and reality of the story of God come to bear upon the person. *Meditatio* is being attentive to what God has done in Christ and the means by which he now by his Spirit calls forth a response from the disciple. "No text can be understood out of its entire context. The most 'entire' context is Jesus. Every biblical text must be read in the living presence of Jesus . . . Meditation discerns the connections and listens for the harmonies that come together in Jesus."[48] *Meditatio* is the moment when an observer of the text becomes a participant with God as directed by his Word. In *meditatio* the meaning of the text becomes clearer, as does an appropriate response to God.

Oratio

From *meditatio* a response begins to form. While prayer is constant throughout all stages of *lectio divina, oratio* is the moment of particular focused prayer. Such a response can be one of intercession, thanksgiving, praise, repentance, adoration, commitment or decision. Such prayer emerges not only from our hearts, but also from the context of the Scripture at hand:

> The Scriptures, read and prayed, are our primary and normative access to God as he reveals himself to us. The Scriptures are our listening post for learning the language of the soul, the ways God speaks to us; they also provide the vocabulary and grammar that are appropriate for us as we in our turn speak to God. Prayer detached from Scripture, from listening to God, disconnected from God's words to us, short-circuits the relational language that is prayer.[49]

As a whole, *lectio divina* is not simply reading Scripture, it is praying *with* Scripture.[50] The key thought to grasp with *oratio* is that, especially in the light of the rich diversity and rawness of the Psalms, any response to God in prayer

---

46. O'Donnell, "Reading for Holiness."
47. Peterson, *Eat This Book*, 101.
48. Ibid., 102.
49. Ibid., 104.
50. Fiedler, "Lectio Divina."

is appropriate. Wrestling with God (Gen 32:22–32; Ps 22) is as reverent as the most poetic and beautifully crafted prayer (Ps 8).

Oratio, as the place of decision and response, is an intersection while ahead lies *contemplatio* and the call to wait on God to receive guidance for how to embody the gospel in the world. The content of *oratio* determines the substance and consequence of this exercise. "*Lectio* [*divina*] has been described as a prayer that begins as a 'dialogue' and ends as a 'duet'. Thus what begins as God addressing us and our responding leads eventually to an experience of union."[51] *Oratio* is also the place of integrity. *Lectio divina* is a process of aligning the person praying with the purposes of God. "The major determinant of prayer or *lectio* is our fidelity to seeking God in everyday behavior. It is no good being fervent in reading if we are slack in living."[52] *Oratio* is that place of intentional response to God in whatever way is most fitting. It can be the place of fierce temptation as in the garden of Eden (Gen 3); the dark wrestling of the garden of Gethsemane (Matt 26); or the joy of the garden of the tomb (John 20). What happens in *oratio*, at least in some measure, impacts upon *contemplatio*.

Contemplatio

Pennington[53] considers the etymology of "contemplation." Elements of the word include ancient Roman terminology concerning a segment of the heavens from which the will of the gods could be discerned, the sense of communion and an abiding state. Pennington arrives at the following definition of contemplation: "to abide with God within his temple."[54] *Contemplatio*, then, means to rest with and be with God with an enhanced sense of his presence. A state of awareness of God is facilitated by the combined effects of having given attention to *lectio*, *meditatio* and *oratio*. This stage of *lectio divina* is the one which depends most upon the gifts and grace of God. "Contemplation can never be seen as the outcome of a process. It remains a gift from God that is not automatically associated with particular human acts."[55] To use two gospel events as analogies: *contemplatio* is the moment of the arrival of

---

51. O'Donnell, "Reading for Holiness," 48.
52. Casey, *Sacred Reading*, 9.
53. Pennington, *Lectio Divina*.
54. Ibid., 65.
55. Casey, *Sacred Reading*, 59.

the cloud on the Mount of Transfiguration as well as the moment when the eyes of the two travellers on the road to Emmaus were opened as Jesus broke the bread.

Contemplatio is best viewed through the lens of the incarnation (John 1:14): "And the Word became flesh and lived [σκηνόω] among us, and we have seen his glory, the glory as of a father's only son, full of grace and truth." *Contemplatio* is both word and action and has the sense of abiding in the context of a temple or tabernacle (σκηνόω); that temple is Christ and the human life. The effect is not removal from the world but intimate involvement with it:

> Contemplative is not an elitist category of Christian . . .
> Contemplative in the context of *lectio divina*, our spiritual reading of the Holy Scriptures, signals recognition of an organic union between the word "read" and the word "lived." The contemplative life is the realization that the Word that was in the beginning is also the Word made flesh and continues to be the Word to which I say, *Fiat mihi*: "Let it be to *me* according to thy Word."[56]

Contemplatio is that moment when we are once again confronted with the incarnation and abide with Christ as he abides in the world (John 17:24). "There is, then, no objective measure of success or failure in the practice of *lectio divina*. The reader is always moving into uncharted waters – a personal encounter with the Word."[57] Thus there can be no precise description given to prepare a person for what might happen in *contemplatio* let alone in *lectio divina* as a whole. God is sovereign and his Spirit moves accordingly (John 3:8).

Ignatian Gospel Contemplation has some similarities with *lectio divina*, such as an emphasis on a close reading of the Scriptures, a personal encounter with them and the contemplative prayerful engagement flavouring it all. However, Ignatian Gospel Contemplation brings a unique contribution in its emphasis on the prayerful transportation of the person into the gospel scene

---

56. Peterson, *Eat This Book*, 113–114, emphasis in original.
57. O'Donnell, "Reading for Holiness," 49–50.

as if they were actually there, and it is that that we will now consider in the second half of this chapter.[58]

Ignatian Gospel Contemplation

Before explaining the specifics of Ignatian Gospel Contemplation, some introductory observations are necessary to orientate the preacher to the context from which this particular prayer emerged. Whereas *lectio divina* is a contained approach to the reading and praying of Scripture, Ignatian Gospel Contemplation is but one aspect of the thirty-day Ignatian retreat known as the Spiritual Exercises.[59] The Exercises developed out of Ignatius of Loyola's spiritual conversion and development. In the first instance he was influenced by reading the *Life of Christ* by Ludolph of Saxony, the *Flos Sanctorum* (*Lives of the Saints*) by Jacobus de Voragine and the *Imitation of Christ* by Thomas à Kempis.[60] However, it is the following quote from an unknown Franciscan in the preface of Ludolph's book which is considered to be the source of Ignatius' use of the imagination in prayer:

> If you wish to draw profit from these meditations, set aside all cares and anxieties. Lovingly and contemplatively, with all the feelings of your heart, make everything that the Lord Jesus said and did present to yourself, just as though you were hearing it with your ears and seeing it with your eyes . . . And even when it is related in the past tense you should contemplate it all as though present today.[61]

Ludolph's work built on this and advanced a form of contemplative prayer which positioned the reader as if they were actually there at the time of Christ. Other types of prayers found in the Exercises had their beginnings in various works of the thirteenth and fifteenth centuries. Indeed, what Guido is to *lectio divina*, Ignatius of Loyola is to imaginative Gospel Contemplation: he created a schema and a context for its use. The Exercises subsequently

---

58. While specifically developed for praying the gospel accounts, Ignatian Gospel Contemplation can be used for any narrative section in Scripture. Hence, as will be evident in chapters 3–5, there were occasions in this research when Old Testament narratives were prayed with the agency of Ignatian Gospel Contemplation.

59. For the purposes of this study, the Spiritual Exercises will be referred to as the Exercises.

60. De Guibert, *The Jesuits*.

61. Rahner, *Ignatius the Theologian*; Walter J. Burghardt, *Long Have I Loved You: A Theologian Reflects on His Church* (New York: Orbis, 2000), 200.

formed the initial training for the order Ignatius established: the Society of Jesus (Jesuits). The Exercises are structured into four weeks during which the life of Christ, as recorded in the Gospels, is contemplated. Each "week" is not necessarily a seven-day period: its duration depends on the progress of the retreatant. No matter how cursory one considers the Exercises, it is clear that the centre of gravity is the intentional contemplation of the divine and human life of Christ.[62] From this basis the Exercises present a person with the presence and love of God, and the challenge of how they will respond to the call of the King.

Consequently, in utilizing Ignatian Gospel Contemplation, this research endeavours to proceed with respect with what is but one part of a larger endeavour. With reference to taking one aspect of the Exercises, Lonsdale states, "[O]ne pitfall is a kind of free-for-all in which a person interpreting a tradition pays little attention to its original context and history but focuses entirely on what it might mean 'for us' today."[63] He continues with the analogy of a director or actor taking a few scenes from *Hamlet* for their own reasons: "the result may or may not be a creative experience, but it is hardly *Hamlet.*"[64] Furthermore, in his book *Ignatius the Theologian*, Hugo Rahner[65] himself focuses on one type of prayer from the Exercises: Application of the Senses. Rahner concedes that this means deliberately bypassing preceding instructions contained in the Exercises and that "this, of course, is just as bad as the anatomical preparation of an organ which can only be fully meaningful in terms of its vital functions within the living entity from which it is taken – but it is a necessary evil at times."[66] Rahner goes on to comment that such an exercise can, however, enlighten the whole. This study, then, endeavours to proceed with the cautions expressed by Lonsdale and Rahner in mind.

While the Exercises contain a number of types of prayer, for the purposes of this study, and in order to appreciate Ignatian Gospel Contemplation, three main types of prayer require comment:

---

62. Rahner, *Ignatius the Theologian*.
63. David Lonsdale, *Eyes to See, Ears to Hear: An Introduction to Ignatian Spirituality*, Traditions of Christian Spirituality, ed. Philip Sheldrake (New York: Orbis, 2000), 22–23.
64. Ibid., 23.
65. Rahner, *Ignatius the Theologian*.
66. Ibid., 182.

Application of the Senses

Application of the Senses was a prayer of review which took place in the evening of each day during the Exercises and was in contrast to any strenuous spiritual work which the day may otherwise have held.[67] "This involves using the imagination to 'see', 'hear', 'feel', 'taste', 'touch', and 'smell' the material prayed over earlier and, as always, to reflect and seek devotion."[68] The Application of the Senses comes into play with the two other types of prayer discussed below. Prayers in the Exercises invariably involve a step referred to as "Composition of the Place," whereby the scene is imagined by calling on the five senses.[69] It needs to be noted that while on the one hand Application of the Senses was a separate exercise, on the other, "there is no adequate distinction between the application of the senses and other methods."[70] The other forms of prayers in the Exercises have the Application of the Senses intrinsically involved.

Discursive Meditations

These are meditations which draw on the three powers of the soul: memory, understanding and the will.[71] These meditations take place mainly in Week One of the Exercises. They tend to pertain "more to reasoning and to what is abstract."[72] Even so, they are softened by the Application of the Senses in the evening of each day during the Exercises. After the first week, the methods of prayer are "easier, simpler and more restful."[73]

Gospel Contemplations

The contemplations on the life of Jesus are the main activity of the Exercises. The retreatant contemplates the events in Jesus' life in chronological order. Week Two focuses on the life and ministry of Jesus, Week Three on the passion, and Week Four on the resurrection. These contemplations are

---

67. Ibid., no page number.

68. Brackley, *Call to Discernment*, 240.

69. Rahner, *Ignatius the Theologian*; Urs Von Balthasar, *The Glory of the Lord: A Theological Aesthetics. Vol. I, Seeing the Form*, edited by John Riches (Edinburgh: T & T Clark, 1982)

70. Brou, *Ignatian Methods of Prayer*, 147.

71. Andre Ravier, *A Do-It-At-Home Retreat: The Spiritual Exercises of St Ignatius of Loyola* (San Francisco: Ignatius Press, 1991).

72. De Guibert, *The Jesuits*, 168.

73. Ibid., 169.

marked by the use of the five physical senses in imagining an event from Jesus' life as recorded in the Gospels. "Ignatian contemplation consists, then, in *reliving the mystery with a great deal of faith and love*; that is, the one who is praying relives the Gospel account as if he were present there and had a part to play in the unfolding mystery."[74] Along with *lectio divina*, it is this form of prayer which will be the focus of this study.

So how does the preacher engage in Ignatian Gospel Contemplation? Prior to the actual contemplation, Ignatius' schema involves a preparatory prayer and three preludes. Each prelude contributes to orientating the person to the Scripture at hand and facilitating the presence of God. Many consider these preludes as adding complexity to the prayer, and consequently various classic and contemporary authors have adapted them in their engagement with the Exercises.[75] The common approach appears to be one of merging the three preludes or "even passing over them in silence."[76] For the purposes of this research project, Brou's contention that the three preludes remain important in orientating a person towards the contemplation was subscribed to.

Preparatory Prayer

To begin, a person quietens their heart and focuses on what is about to take place and why. This involves consciously placing themselves in the presence of God and being aware of the love of God towards them.

First Prelude: Subject Matter

In the first prelude the passage of Scripture is read and re-read any number of times so that the story is absorbed. The purpose is to gain an overall orientation of the subject matter.

Second Prelude: Composition of Place

Then, relying on the description from Scripture, the imagination is used to compose the scene for contemplation. The five physical senses are employed to build the scene. In the Exercises Ignatius would provide brief prompts to excite the imagination. For instance, for the contemplation of the birth of Christ, he writes:

---

74. Ravier, *A Do-It-At-Home Retreat*, 39, emphasis in original.
75. Brou, *Ignatian Methods of Prayer*.
76. Ibid., 94.

This is a mental representation of the place. It will consist here in seeing in imagination the way from Nazareth to Bethlehem. Consider its length, its breadth; whether level, or through valleys and over hills. Observe also the place or cave where Christ is born; whether big or little; whether high or low; and how it is arranged.[77]

Liberty of expression is an important feature of Ignatian spirituality; however, appropriate accuracy in the composition of place is salutary. "The composition of place should be made, so to say, in the spirit of prayer."[78] The spirit of the prayer ought to be in harmony with the event and scene being imagined. For instance, while horror and despair would mark contemplation of the crucifixion, joy and wonder would mark contemplation of the resurrection.

Third Prelude: Asking for the Desired Grace

This is a prayer whereby a person entrusts himself or herself to the grace of God, asking, in the words of Ignatius, "for the grace that all my intentions, actions, and operations may be ordered purely to the service and praise of his Divine Majesty."[79] Throughout the Exercises the desired grace asked for ranges from "an intimate knowledge of our Lord"[80] to "sorrow, compassion, and shame because the Lord is going to His suffering for my sins."[81] The specific grace requested will vary from person to person, depending on the material being contemplated and the current circumstances the person is experiencing.[82] It may appear that to ask for specific grace pre-empts and attempts to engineer the outcome of the prayer. However, it was recognized that it was one thing to request a particular grace but quite another as to how the Holy Spirit might answer that request. Ignatius' thinking was that the asking for grace was due to the influence of God in any case. He writes,

---

77. Excerpt from *The Spiritual Exercises of St. Ignatius of Loyola* by Louis J. Puhl, S. J. (Newman Press 1951), 43, ann 112. The abbreviation "ann" means "annotation" and is the convention for referencing the numbered sections in the Exercises. By way of example, the full text of the nativity contemplation is contained in appendix A. Reprinted with permission of Loyola Press. To order copies of this book call 1-800-621-1008 (USA) or go to www.loyolapress.com.

78. Brou, *Ignatian Methods of Prayer*, 98.

79. Puhl, *Spiritual Exercises of St Ignatius*, 21, ann 46.

80. Ibid., 42, ann 104.

81. Ibid., 63, ann 193.

82. Brou, *Ignatian Methods of Prayer*.

"What I so much desire I shall not labor to obtain through my own effort, but I shall ask for it, because I know I can do nothing. Under the impulse of grace which makes me feel my need, I ask God to give me that which I cannot help desiring."[83] The presence of God is assumed at every stage of the prayer and his guidance depended upon constantly.

Gospel Contemplation

Having engaged with the three preludes, the person now begins the contemplation itself. Brackley puts it succinctly when he writes that we should "allow the story to unfold in our imagination like a film."[84] Once the contemplation commences "we enter the story . . . considering above all the people involved: we (1) observe them, (2) listen to what they say, and (3) note what they do (not necessarily in that order), reflecting on what promises to bear fruit."[85] So a person enters the story and, in the same way as with poetry or a novel, allows their imagination to be touched by the biblical event.[86] Ignatius lists points which serve as direction for the one praying. Such points include which character to assume in the contemplation, what to listen for and what to observe. The person praying decides which role they will take in the playing out of the biblical event. Whether they are a central character, a member of the crowd or an observer at a distance is a matter of personal preference.

Colloquy

Once a person has contemplated the event from Scripture, the contemplation finishes with a conversation or discussion with Christ, regardless of how the contemplation is considered to have gone.[87] The subject for the colloquy is whatever has transpired in the preceding contemplation, and the conversation is conducted "in the way one friend speaks to another, or a servant to one in authority."[88] Authenticity is crucial in the colloquy:

> In the colloquy I ought always to speak and pray *according to the actual state of my soul*. In other words, whether I am tempted or

---

83. Quoted in Brou, *Ignatian Methods of Prayer*, 104.

84. Brackley, *Call to Discernment*, 239.

85. Ibid.

86. William A. Barry, *Letting God Come Close: An Approach to the Ignatian Spiritual Exercises* (Chicago: Loyola Press, 2001).

87. Ravier, *A Do-It-At-Home Retreat*.

88. Quoting ann 54, Brackley, *Call to Discernment*, 74.

fervent, whether I want this virtue or that, whether I want to get ready to make a particular commitment, or whether I want to be sad or joyful in the mystery I am contemplating – the point is that I should never divorce my here-and-now self from my conversation in the colloquy.[89]

The colloquy is especially important as this dialogue with Christ is marked with an increasing awareness of how the effect of the prayer will translate into contemporary life.

It may appear that the outline of Ignatian Gospel Contemplation is formulaic and marked by constraint. However, the Exercises are marked by freedom, generosity of spirit and an appreciation of the preferences, circumstances and abilities of individual retreatants.[90] While the contemplations are powerfully rooted in the Word, "what is striking throughout [the Exercises] is the liberty given to retreatants to allow their imagination full rein. There is no attempt whatsoever to control the retreatant's reflection through any biblical data not bearing immediately upon the purpose of the meditation."[91] Ignatius' own counsel in this matter included the following: "God sees and knows what is best for us, and as He knows all, He points out the way to follow. But we, even with His grace, have a hard time finding it, and may have to try several ways before we travel by that which is evidently the one for us."[92]

Jesuit luminaries after Ignatius continued to advance such liberty of spirit. Indeed, as can be observed in the text of instructions concerning the nativity contemplation (appendix A), details are scarce even though Ignatius had been to the Holy Land. He does not impose a scene upon a person's own imagination.[93] Directors of the Exercises were instructed to give only brief descriptions to the retreatants. This was to create space for the retreatant and not clutter their heart and mind with too much information. "What Ignatius is requiring of the retreatant throughout the Exercises is, above all, an exercise of the imagination."[94] Byrne adds further: "Ignatius believed very strongly that in achieving the conversion and freedom, which are the main aim of the

---

89. Ravier, *A Do-It-At-Home Retreat,* 33, emphasis in original.

90. Andre Ravier, *Ignatius Loyola and the Founding of the Society of Jesus* (San Francisco: Ignatius Press, 1987); *A Do-It-At-Home Retreat*; Lonsdale, *Eyes to See, Ears to Hear.*

91. Byrne, "To See with the Eyes," 6.

92. Brou, *Ignatian Methods of Prayer,* 24.

93. Barry, *Letting God Come Close.*

94. Byrne, "To See with the Eyes," 5.

Exercises, the imagination was where the contest was chiefly engaged. The more active and less passive the retreatant could be in this process, so much the better."[95]

People's imaginations, and their ability to use them, vary greatly from one person to another. Some people may "see" a lot, others may "hear" a lot, and still others experience discouragement from their apparent paucity of imagination.[96] "Imaginations differ, and we need to let God use the one we have and not bemoan the one we do not have."[97] With particular reference to the second prelude, Brou observes that "the composition of place is good [not] only for a fairly lively imagination, but one that is normal and under the control of serious common sense."[98] Hence Brou captures the wisdom of Ignatian spirituality which has high expectations of an encounter with God and is garnished with healthy pragmatism.

Definitions: Meditation and Contemplation

Misunderstandings and suspicions concerning meditation and contemplation are common. Such misunderstandings are exacerbated by the tendency for the terms to be used interchangeably and without distinction. *Lectio divina* and Ignatian Gospel Contemplation are predicated on a clear understanding of the nuances and nature of meditation and contemplation. For the purposes of this research, the definitions of meditation and contemplation as contained in the Catholic catechism are subscribed to. The following extracts capture the essence of the definitions of both terms as contained in the catechism:

> **Meditation** is a prayerful quest engaging thought, imagination, emotion, and desire. Its goal is to make our own in faith the subject considered, by confronting it with the reality of our own life.

> **Contemplative prayer** is the simple expression of the mystery of prayer. It is a gaze of faith fixed on Jesus, an attentiveness to the Word of God, a silent love. It achieves real union with the prayer of Christ to the extent that it makes us share in his mystery.

---

95. Ibid., 6.

96. Barry, *Letting God Come Close.*

97. Ibid., 102.

98. Brou, *Ignatian Methods of Prayer*, 100.

Meditation

Meditation is above all a quest. The mind seeks to understand the why and how of the Christian life, in order to adhere to and respond to what the Lord is asking.

Christians owe it to themselves to develop the desire to meditate regularly, lest they come to resemble the three first kinds of soil in the parable of the sower. But a method is only a guide; the important thing is to advance, with the Holy Spirit, along the one way of prayer: Christ Jesus.

Contemplation

What is contemplative prayer?

- St Teresa answers: "Contemplative prayer in my opinion is nothing else than a close sharing between friends; it means taking time frequently to be alone with him who we know loves us." Contemplative prayer seeks him "whom my soul loves." It is Jesus, and in him, the Father.
- Contemplation is a gaze of faith, fixed on Jesus. "I look at him and he looks at me." This focus on Jesus is a renunciation of self.[99]

Meditation and Contemplation in *Lectio Divina* and Ignatian Gospel Contemplation

While the above-mentioned definitions of meditation and contemplation capture the spirit and intent of the two disciplines at hand, it is necessary to discuss the particular expression of both in the exercise of the two prayer disciplines. At risk of over-simplifying *lectio divina*, we can say that the difference between *meditatio* and *contemplatio* is that the former is an exercise in analysis whereas the latter is an exercise in receptivity. *Contemplatio* has been likened to two people who are in love simply sitting in the wordless company of each other and basking in the warmth of being known and loved

---

99. US Catholic Church, ed., *Catechism of the Catholic Church* (New York: Doubleday, 1995), 713–715.

deeply.[100] It does need to be acknowledged, though, that Guido did articulate a progression which presented *contemplatio* as being attained by a select few. He "speaks of reading as belonging to the beginners, meditation to the proficient, prayer to the devoted, and contemplation to the blessed."[101] Also, various contemporary writers[102] echo this and speak of *contemplatio* as potentially including a rarefied spiritual experience. For example: "Contemplation is the summit of the prayer experience, a profound communion with God that is all-embracing and changes one's life, perhaps dramatically. Such experiences are rare but not impossible for the beginner."[103] However, Peterson posits that it is erroneous to consider *contemplatio* as a form of advanced meditation attained by very few.[104] While *contemplatio* can involve intense and dramatic experiences of God, so can any of the previous three elements of *lectio divina*. Dwyer puts the issue thus:

> *Contemplatio* was translated as "contemplation" and then you were told, "But contemplation is only for chosen souls like myself [a Trappist priest] and others who are called to contemplative monasteries. The rest of you poor people are called only to meditate and that is the way it is. Too bad. Some are chosen, some aren't." It's a heresy.[105]

Dwyer comments further that meditation was then viewed as the simple alternative while contemplation remained supposedly only within reach of very gifted mystics. Thus people used this as an excuse not to engage in contemplation, and this "was a tragedy in the history of the Church."[106] My view is that it is within the realm of all who seek Christ in prayer, but that teaching and discipline in its application are necessary. A rounded understanding of contemplation is important, therefore, as is an appreciation of what is meant by it. However, regardless of the form which contemplation may take, it always remains in the realm of grace and is a gift from God.

---

100. Luke Dysinger, "Accepting the Embrace of God: The Ancient Art of Lectio Divina," Valyermo Benedictine, accessed 3 June 2009 on http://www.valyermo.com/ld-art.html. David L. Miller, "Lectio Divina Divine Reading," The Lutheran, December 2003, accessed 3 June 2009 at http://www.thelutheran.org/article/article.cfm?article_id=3470.

101. Egan, "Guigo II," 114.

102. O'Donnell, "Reading for Holiness"; Casey, *Sacred Reading*; Pennington, *Lectio Divina*.

103. O'Donnell, "Reading for Holiness," 49.

104. Peterson, *Eat This Book*.

105. Dwyer, "Many Paths to Prayer."

106. Ibid.

With reference to Ignatian Gospel Contemplation, precision concerning the definition of the two terms is also required. Brackley provides a succinct summary:

> In the Exercises, Ignatius distinguishes between discursive meditation and imaginative contemplation. In the former we think more; we remember, ponder, strive to understand . . . We would meditate over a passage of Paul's letter to the Romans in this way . . . For Ignatius, "contemplation" means imaginatively re-creating a scene from the gospels or some other story, reliving it in our imagination and reflecting on it.[107]

Yet, just as there is a sense of integration and cross-pollination between the elements of *lectio divina*, so there is within the different types of prayers in the Exercises. On the one hand, they stand alone; on the other, they share an interdependence:

> It is not a mere accident that the words *meditation* and *contemplation* are employed in the Exercises. A scene from the life of Christ is never "meditated," but "contemplated." Assuredly, the Ignatian contemplation of these scenes is discursive prayer, but in its movement it is less reasoning and abstract, and more direct, concrete, restful, and affective. Too much overlooking of this fact has sometimes caused the Exercises to be regarded as a mere office-machine for reasoning.[108]

Indeed, it needs to be acknowledged that it is actually easier to experience contemplation than describe it.[109] Ignatius himself also speaks of such elusiveness in trying to explain contemplation pending a person actually experiencing it.[110] Contemplation is the fuel for activity in the world as a result of learning "the 'interior knowledge of our Lord', the more to love him and follow him." The hope of this study was to reflect on the experience of participants as to whether their contemplation *had* led them to love and follow Christ in the world. Indeed, practical post-contemplation activity is presumed by Ignatian Gospel Contemplation and *lectio divina*. "While the Christian life ostensibly consists in alternative periods of action and

---

107. Brackley, *Call to Discernment*, 237, 239.
108. Joseph De Guibert, *The Jesuits*, 135, n 41, emphasis in original.
109. Merton, *Seeds of Contemplation*.
110. Rahner, *Ignatius the Theologian*.

contemplation, its aim should be to make the two interpenetrate more and more."[111] Insofar as this remains unrecognized, it is an injustice to the spiritual practice of contemplation. This lack of recognition advances the myth that to be contemplative means to be withdrawn and absent from the world.

Contemplatives in Action

This research's overarching hypothesis is that the exercise of *lectio divina* and Ignatian Gospel Contemplation noticeably affect the ministry of preaching. Contemplation's part in that is not passive:

> There is an active life which proceeds from the fullness of contemplation, such as teaching and preaching . . . And this work is more excellent than simple contemplation. For even as it is better to enlighten than merely shine, so it is better to give to others the fruits of one's contemplation than merely to contemplate.[112]

Such post-contemplation activity, and all other actions motivated by the experience of contemplation, is representative of the Ignatian term *contemplatives in action.* This translates as living with the sense that the world is a sacrament[113] and seeing reality as God does. It means perceiving how God works, listening to his call and embracing the gifts he presents to us, no matter through whom or by what form they come.[114] "This new perception of reality is included in what Jeronimo Nadal (d. 1580), one of the first Jesuits, called being 'a contemplative in action.'"[115] The aim of the Exercises was to facilitate "contemplatives in action." Brackley explains:

> *Contemplativus in actione,* yes. But a more exact formulation of what Ignatius had in mind would be *united to God in seeking and doing God's will.* We are united to God not by prayer as such but by seeking and doing what God wants. Sometimes this means praying. More often it means some other kind of activity. A Jesuit

---

111. Hans Urs von Balthasar, *Essays in Theology II: Word and Redemption* (New York: Herder & Herder, 1965), 123.

112. Brou, *Ignatian Methods of Prayer*, 28.

113. Lonsdale, *Eyes to See, Ears to Hear.*

114. Antonio Guillen, "Imitating Christ Our Lord with the Senses: Senses and Feeling in the Exercises," *The Way* 47, nos 1 and 2 (2008).

115. Ibid., 238.

told Ignatius that he found God primarily in solitude and by meditating or praying privately. Ignatius responded, "What do you mean? Do you draw no profit from helping your neighbor? For this is our practice."[116]

Barry puts the nature of contemplation in Ignatian thought succinctly: "What was the original genial insight of Ignatius of Loyola? I would say that it was the idea that God can be found in all things, that every human experience has a religious dimension and religious meaning."[117] In particular, such awareness always had an edge in that it was a pursuit in discerning and obeying the will of God.

To consider contemplation and action as either/or is erroneous. Contemplation leads to action, and in turn action nourishes contemplation.[118] Several explanations and illustrations are helpful in illuminating the organic relationship they enjoy with each other. While writing with specific reference to contemplation and *lectio divina*, Dysinger[119] speaks of the ancient understanding of and approach to contemplation as an oscillation between practice and prayer. Both were considered as two poles of the same spiritual rhythm, with movement between spiritual activity and receptivity. The spiritual activity related to activity within the heart rather than apostolic action. Dysinger goes on to point out that the early monastic tradition understood contemplation in two ways. There was contemplation of God in creation (God in "the many") and contemplation of God in himself (God as "The One"). By contemplating God as "The One," *lectio divina* then enabled a person to contemplate God "in the many." Yet at the pole of receptivity, contemplation is enjoyed as the sheer gift of God, void of activity but a simple resting in his presence. As Brou states, "[T]he soul gazes without reasoning. She delights in what faith offers her, in what hope presents to her, in what she clasps in charity."[120] Luminaries such as Thomas Aquinas and Jerome Nadal illustrated the relationship between contemplation and action by using the story of Mary and Martha (Luke 10:38–42) as an analogy and calling for a combination of their qualities.[121] A further explanation focuses on the person

---

116. Brackley, *Call to Discernment*, 245, emphasis in original.

117. Barry, *Letting God Come Close*, 91.

118. Brou, *Ignatian Methods of Prayer*.

119. Dysinger, Luke. "Accepting the Embrace of God."

120. Brou, *Ignatian Methods of Prayer*, 155–156.

121. Ibid.

and work of Christ. "Christ's contemplation consists in his being the Word of the *Father*, his action in his being the *Word* of the Father. 'I speak that which I have seen with my Father' (Jn 8:38)."[122] The life of Jesus consistently modelled the rhythm and integration of a life which expressed contemplation in action. Von Balthasar further places Jesus' expression of this by describing it in the context of eternity: "The whole time of the Lord on earth can be considered action that flows from the fullness of his heavenly and eternal contemplation, and returns to it."[123] Hence, there is the sense that contemplation in action truly advances and embraces the theological significance of the incarnation. To be a *contemplative in action* guards against two extremes: fleeing into the world in action but without the empowerment of God, or fleeing from the world and not being present in it.[124] To be a *contemplative in action* means to be incarnational, empowered by the Spirit of Christ.

This chapter began by referring to the unsuspecting disciples' encounter with Christ on the Mount of Transfiguration (Mark 9:2–8) and the road to Emmaus (Luke 24:13–35). These two incidents were held up as a template for the potential outcomes of praying the Scriptures with *lectio divina* and Ignatian Gospel Contemplation. Both prayer disciplines facilitate a face-to-face encounter with the Word of God (John 1:1–5; Heb 1:1–2), written and living. They enable a person to immerse himself or herself in the Word so that the transcendence (Mount of Transfiguration) and immanence (road to Emmaus) of God can be experienced. They orientate the contemporary disciple of Christ to the primacy of Scripture and the agency of the Spirit in the pursuit of responding to God. Both have served the purposes of God and his church for centuries. Today, pastoral leaders are under extraordinary pressure to ensure that the churches they lead are growing, appealing and relevant. The Christian marketplace peddles all manner of programmes, with many having salvific and messianic status bestowed upon them and promising to deliver extraordinary results to stressed-out pastors. The terrible and cumulative cost of lurching from one offer to another is that in the sincere attempt to be relevant to the wider world, the church loses its distinctiveness. In contrast, prayerful attention to the Scriptures through the use of these two

---

122. Von Balthasar, *Essays in Theology II*, 118, emphasis in original.

123. Ibid., 119.

124. Emmanuel Da Silva e Araujo, "Ignatian Spirituality as a Spirituality of Incarnation," *The Way Supplement* 47, nos 1 and 2 (2008).

prayer disciplines, which have been treasured throughout church history, may well form churches which are relevantly distinctive. The result could be that those who defy the equivalent of Christian infomercials and instead immerse themselves in Scripture might relive another unexpected biblical encounter with God: the road to Damascus (Acts 9:1–19). May we be converted again and have the scales fall from our eyes.

3

Renewal

We now turn our attention to the results of this research exercise. The method employed is outlined in detail in appendix B. Eight vocational preachers (including the author) agreed to utilize the two prayer disciplines as part of their regular sermon preparation week by week over a four-month period. Each preacher would preach at least ten sermons during this time and *lectio divina* and Ignatian Gospel Contemplation would be utilized a minimum of three times each. Each preacher would exercise their own discretion as to which prayer discipline to use for the balance of the four remaining sermons. Hence the data for this research is based on at least eighty sermons.

The findings emerged as ten main themes evident from the participants' discussions during the six meetings held (November 2009, February–June 2010). These ten themes cluster into three groups and lead naturally one into another. A chapter is dedicated to each cluster in turn. This chapter addresses the first cluster of themes which describe initial positive experiences, specifically the recovery of the primacy of preaching in the participants' ministries, the preachers' sense of authenticity and a new depth of engagement with the Scriptures. Chapter 4 addresses the second cluster of themes, which delve into the participants' concerns and those elements which helped alleviate their struggles. The themes contained in this cluster are the effects of pastoral demands, the difficulty in determining appropriate content for the sermon post-prayer, the aid of a particular feature of Ignatian Gospel Contemplation, and the place of exegesis in it all. Chapter 5 addresses the final group of themes: a new connection with participants' congregations, the development of the imagination, and movement into the world. We begin, then, with considering the first cluster of themes.

Recovering from a Perceived Loss

The first theme was almost immediately evident from the moment the group convened the first time for the training day (17 November 2009). All seven[1] participants had volunteered for this research exercise motivated by a desire to recapture their first love of preaching the Scriptures to the people of God. This theme emerged prominently as a result of the participants' reflecting on the various forces at work within the pastoral contexts in which they preach. These forces included a consumer mentality within congregations and a lack of biblical literacy, which sometimes resulted in a backlash to biblical sermons. In response to these issues, all seven participants attested to a desire to take advantage of professional development in preaching in order to be better equipped to rise above such pressures. However, as Bob (twenty-seven years in Presbyterian ministry), Helen (ten years as an Anglican vicar) and Josie (in her fifth year as a Baptist pastor) lamented, such opportunities were rare, and those opportunities which were available were often little more than pragmatic fads. Hence, the presence of negative forces and the paucity of ongoing training opportunities culminated in an erosion of the participants' primary focus on preaching. There was a distinct sense within the group that this crucial expression of their pastoral ministry needed recovery and that their involvement in this research was an attempt to rectify the problem they were experiencing. Even Kathy, who had only been in ordained ministry seven months, articulated a strong desire to galvanize her call and confidence to preach. Furthermore, there was an associated facet to the theme of loss of attention to the primacy of preaching. The rigours and pressures of pastoral ministry eroded not only group members' attention to the preaching ministry but also their personal attention to the Scriptures and their own spiritual growth.

This second aspect of loss – attention to personal spiritual growth – was expressed in terms of the struggle to simultaneously execute a professional preaching ministry and attend to personal devotions. The occupational hazard of dealing with the Scriptures was lamented by Kathy, who said, "[As I have completed more formal study] I find it more difficult to know 'Lord, how do I connect with you in a devotional way?'" The pitfalls of handling Scripture as

---

1. This research mainly reports on the experiences of the seven research participants rather than the author. The author's experiences are included in the final reflections in the concluding chapter.

professionals, as described by Merton, Burghardt, Schneiders and Thurston,[2] and cited in chapter 1, were attested to by all seven participants. However, three participants advocated the use of sermon preparation doubling as a time for personal devotions. This contribution had a positive effect upon the group, especially upon Kathy, and set up an expectation that the two prayer disciplines could facilitate both a personal encounter for the preacher during sermon preparation and a public message for the congregations. Josie accurately summed up the heart of the group's starting point and hoped-for destination when she said, "We are all keen to nourish ourselves in order to nourish others."

While fulfilment of the hope to recover their first love for preaching and to experience spiritual growth gently punctuated the whole research phase, participants especially noted its presence in the early and later stages of the exercise. When the group met for the second time (February 2010), four participants reported an increased sense of energy and a recovery of their passion for preaching. Helen referred to the change as a return of "fire in the belly," which was also the phrase her congregation used when giving her feedback. She had preached three times, and claimed that the congregation's feedback for two of those sermons was the best she had received in a long time.

In the intervening period from this early stage to the last meeting (June 2010), signs of recovery subtly underscored the other nine themes as participants described their discoveries and even their struggles. However, it was not until the final meeting, when participants revisited their initial reasons for engaging with the research, that the presence of the recovery was particularly realized and celebrated. All group members present spoke not only of having been re-orientated to their call as preachers, but also of having their understanding of that call enriched. Michael (a Presbyterian minister with seven years experience) reported enthusiastically how the process had revealed that there was "really something missing in my preaching and in the way I engage with Scripture," and that he had achieved his goal of recovering his first love. Gwen (a Methodist minister with fifteen years experience) and Josie spoke of how the two prayer disciplines had heightened their awareness of the presence and sovereignty of God in the pursuit of the call to preach, even when the prayers appeared not to bear fruit. Josie had hoped that the two prayer disciplines would prove to be "fail-proof formulas," but had instead

---

2. Merton, *Opening the Bible*; Burghardt, *Preaching*; Schneiders, "Biblical Spirituality"; Thurston, "On Biblical Preaching."

found that they "*reinforced* what a precarious business the whole preaching, sermon prep, sermon delivery, sermon process is; you're always working at it. But you're never finding *the way* that works."[3]

The recovery of their first love included the stripping away of unrealistic expectations, an enhancement of the sense of God's presence and the nature of their call being deepened. For example, in an email sent by Frank (a Baptist pastor for twelve years) after the final meeting, he used Acts 6:1–7 ("attention to prayer and ministry of the Word") as a template to describe the change in him. He had previously considered that a pastor needed to be found praying and to be found preaching, but that the two activities were mutually exclusive. He is now convinced that the two are inseparable. *In lieu* of attending the last meeting, Bob emailed, "I have recaptured the significance of preaching as an essential part of the life of the church . . . The most significant discovery has been a reawakening of the place and value of well-prepared preaching in the life of the Christian community."[4] By the end of the research period, *lectio divina* and Ignatian Gospel Contemplation placed all the participants in an arena by means of which their first love for God and preaching could be revisited and revived. The renewal of the group members' first love for God and for preaching, and as that pertained to the congregations they served, resulted in a growing sense of authenticity in the moment of sermon delivery – an aspect to which we now turn.

Authenticity of the Preacher

In the introduction to this book we quoted Phillips Brooks' definition of preaching: "truth through personality."[5] In the light of Brooks' definition, one hypothesis of this research was that *lectio divina* and Ignatian Gospel Contemplation would facilitate a greater sense of personal authenticity in the preacher. The expectation was that the preacher would experience a personal encounter with God during sermon preparation which would be evident in the content and delivery of that sermon. Such a change would be predicated on the Spirit of Christ at work during the preacher's prayerful engagement with the text and the preacher becoming more aware of the reality of the incarnation and their preaching context. While not all

---

3. Italics are used to signify a group participant's emphasis of a word or phrase.

4. All group members had been sent the list of questions in preparation for the last meeting. However, Bob was unable to attend, due to a family emergency.

5. Brooks, *Phillips Brooks on Preaching*, 8.

participants could say that they had become especially aware of the reality of the incarnation per se, they all consistently described a new experience of being personally arrested by the text and more present when they preached it. The observation was made by Josie and Kathy that the "personality [of the preacher] and the responsibility of preaching" came closer together. This realization enhanced the sense of personal investment and presence in the task of sermon preparation. For example, Helen preached from John 20:19–31 about the disciples' post-resurrection fear. She made the telling contrast between preparing a sermon which had involved her personally examining whether she herself was living in a locked room (John 20:19), and her normal *modus operandi* of "just organizing it [the sermon] for 500 other people." The engagement with the Scriptures caught the participants in a vortex of involvement that emphasized, as Josie said, the "responsibility to really keep developing personally and engaging personally so that everything is coming through my personality, not a pragmatic series of steps." The Scriptures formed the preacher's personality through the use of these prayers so that, as Gwen memorably observed, the "Spirit got into those crevices." The imperative "pray, so God will be able to preach through you"[6] is an accurate way to describe the effect. The preacher became more of a conduit for the message of Scripture.

While a new sense of authenticity permeated the whole period of time, Easter proved to be an occasion which particularly amplified this finding. The participants became witnesses of the passion and resurrection of Christ. They were greatly moved by these gospel events and were powerfully compelled to tell their congregations about them. Of the nine sermons preached by the group on Palm Sunday and Easter Sunday, eight utilized Ignatian Gospel Contemplation.[7] The effect was still evident two weeks later when the group convened and Helen breathlessly shared, "But actually I felt engaged with it. Actually I engaged with a process in this and I found a moment that 'God, this is *amazing*. This is *absolutely amazing*.' And felt that's what I had to tell my community. And thought, 'Thank you, God, for the gift of this process that led me to that point.'"

They really did seem to possess a persona of having been present in the gospel accounts so that they preached as eyewitnesses. The comment

---

6. Susan Jones, "The Purpose of Preaching," *Candour* (2010): 11.

7. Two group members did not preach during Easter and a third member, Frank, was on his honeymoon. That meant that five group members, including myself (the author), preached during this time.

was made that the oft-used word to describe evangelism is "witnessing"; however, it appears that this term's genesis has been largely forgotten by the contemporary Christian community. Its original use described the mandate of the first disciples who bore witness that Christ who died had now been raised from the dead. Today its definition tends to be more generic and refers to the explanation of the tenets of faith in order that a person might be converted to Christ. While this is appropriate, an edge is lost if this is detached from being grounded in bearing personal witness to the resurrection. The effect of the sermons preached by the group was to bring the resurrection front and centre as by those who had somehow witnessed it, an effect which transcended just a seasonal observation. While there is evidence that all those who preached during Easter were more conspicuous in the sermon content by virtue of increased fervour and personal bearing, it was pleasing to note that the attendant danger of the preacher becoming too prominent was absent. In fact, the participants proved very diligent in self-policing whether a sermon was becoming too autobiographical. Helen commented that she did not think the congregation knew anything more about her as a person as a result of one of the Easter sermons, but rather that the prayer discipline "empowers what I'm saying, what I saw." However, there is an inescapable cost to experiencing Scripture by being personally drawn into the biblical story and then preaching a message in its aftermath. On the occasions when it was deemed appropriate to include autobiographical material there were pronounced moments when the preacher experienced feelings of marked vulnerability.

The genesis of such vulnerability was that as group members were immersed in Scripture in prayer, they experienced a new sense of honesty and uncharacteristic candidness with God. The common form of vulnerability centred on the struggle as to how to communicate this divine encounter with their congregations. When such material was included, the preacher described it as vulnerability, while the congregation described it as powerful. Several participants reported that the particular point of the contemplation which struck them most personally translated to the corresponding point in the sermon which had the most effect upon the congregation. Early in the process, Frank described this phenomenon as "*hugely* worthwhile." He went on to say, "I think that one of the struggles I've had for years really is the desire that there will be something of the Spirit in the preparation of this stuff that will touch people's lives and my life. And that is an infrequent occurrence. But in these last two messages I could pinpoint it."

By way of example, Kathy was preparing a sermon on Joseph's reconciliation with his brothers (Gen 50:15–21). All the commentaries she consulted posited different reasons for the evidence of tears in the account. Such a diversity of opinion was of little help, so through the use of Ignatian Gospel Contemplation Kathy engaged with the story to encounter the tears. It was this moment of prayer and the resultant form it took in the sermon as she spoke of the feelings experienced which connected most powerfully with people.

Frank said he had only ever thought of preaching in terms of power, and it was not until Kathy spoke of the vulnerability that he saw it in an entirely new light. This resulted in new categories and vocabulary for the group to plumb their experiences.

The growth in the sense of authenticity was also experienced in the form of a new degree of discernment. As mentioned earlier in this chapter, one of the pressures confronting participants in their preaching ministry was the paucity of opportunities for professional development. At times this vacuum is filled by an overwhelming plethora of preaching wares and approaches which often amount to pragmatic fads. The difficulty is to know which ones are valuable innovations and which are attention-grabbing gimmicks. In particular, Bob made mention of the growing call for preachers to subscribe more to multimedia presentations, to depart from the traditional sole-preacher format and to embrace a more dialogical and discussion forum *in lieu* of the classical sermon. Instead of such calls unsettling the group members and tempting them to abandon conventional preaching approaches, the discovery was made that these methods were overshadowed by the prayer disciplines which the group described as genuine for the preacher and their congregation. Bob expanded on this thought:

> When you've been preaching for quite a while there is that danger . . . of looking for that quirky sort of approach. Or that new way of looking at that oh-so-familiar passage when you get to certain key times of the year or whatever. But actually I think hanging in with the process [*lectio divina* and Ignatian Gospel Contemplation] is a far more reliable way of actually hearing something that you may not expect . . . You're looking for that symbol or that illustration or that story that will really wow people. But actually this is more genuine, what I'm hearing. If you hold on to it, it's actually *far* more genuine and real.

The effect of praying *lectio divina* and Ignatian Gospel Contemplation was to enable the preacher to decide what would now best serve in communicating the message effectively. The preacher was now able to engage with new ideas concerning the practice of preaching from a place which was primarily created through a searching engagement with the Scriptures. On one occasion a sermon of Bob's did become very dialogical when it was preached. In fact, the main dialogical partner during the sermon was a Muslim who was visiting that day. The point is that through the use of the prayer disciplines preachers can become less reactionary and insecure, grasping at the latest trend and losing their preaching soul in the process. The prayerful process of placing the preacher in the Scriptures leads them on to making prudent decisions as to what to adopt from current thinking for the sermon at hand.

This growth in discernment emerged from a renewed confidence in the Scriptures and a corresponding confidence in the participants themselves. This aspect of authenticity proved the most prominent throughout the time of research. The effect of this confidence flavours many of the findings from this research and will be evident in subsequent sections and chapters. This development of confidence enabled all seven participants to go beyond their training in exegesis without abandoning it. Some reported a frustration, attributed to their formal theological training, which caused them to think that in approaching a passage of Scripture they ought to make the same observations as anyone else studying the same passage. However, through the agency of *lectio divina* and Ignatian Gospel Contemplation the Word of God became more immediate to the preacher and consequently to their congregation. This generated the confidence to grapple with the text, craft a message and bring it to the congregation. It facilitated more confidence in the preacher so that they felt that the value of their insights was not dependent on which commentary was consulted but on the fact that they had encountered God through his Word. In the final group meeting this sense of confidence was still being highlighted and celebrated, as illustrated by this comment of Josie's:

> . . . I think that confidence also links to me discovering how I think about, feel about, respond to a text – is *really* important and valuable for me in my context and congregation. And I have had really positive experiences of the process in that I think I have made my sermons a bit more relevant than they were in the past because I've found that confidence to talk to *our* context and my experience of a text and trying to apply that to us all.

As mentioned above, the conventions of exegesis were still attended to, but now "truth through personality" was being liberated in a new way. This deepening sense of authenticity was predicated on habitually dwelling with the text – and we now turn our attention to further findings in this regard.

Dwelling with the Text

The experience of all seven group members was that the two prayer disciplines facilitated a distinct change in their relationship with the Scriptures. Terms used to describe the change include the sense of Scripture becoming "rich" and "alive." As Frank put it, he "learned how to inhabit the text, not just use it." The phrase which gained prominence within the group and which summarizes the change is "dwelling with the text." Group members testified to slowing down when reading Scripture and essentially taking up residence in the passage at hand. Such careful and intentional focus on the text, or dwelling with the text, formed the foundation upon which the aforementioned authenticity and confidence rested. There was a wonderful symmetry and outworking of the incarnation in the group's experience. They were incarnate in the text and experienced the incarnation. They dwelt with Christ through his Word and were able to identify, or at least glimpse, Christ in turn dwelling with his people through the subsequent preaching of the Word. Kathy said, "You are experiencing a new incarnation each time you perform the role [preaching]. There is power carrying it out. I think it is the power of the Scripture and the interaction with God's people." Their experience parallels Heisler's exhortation:

> As a preacher, you are an incarnate testimony of what your text is saying. People in the audience can see that you have been with Jonah in the belly of the great fish. They can smell the decaying body of Lazarus as you preach Jesus, the resurrection and the life. They hear the screams of the demoniac as you paint the picture of unceasing torment in the text. They taste the anguish of the Passover meal that Jesus shared with his disciples. It's not so much that you transport your audience back to Mary and Martha's first-century house but rather that you visit in their house long enough so that your audience senses you have been there yourself.[8]

---

8. Heisler, *Spirit-led Preaching*, 98.

By way of example, my experience during this research involved preaching a sermon from Amos 1–2. Through dwelling with the text my preaching was uncharacteristically passionate and intense. The sermon content centred on the fire of God and judgement, and while I was genuinely myself, I was markedly different. At the end of the sermon I gave an opportunity for the congregation to come forward and light a candle in response. This in itself was a rare invitation, and so many people responded that they had to form a queue. The extraordinary aspect of the feedback was that people spoke of the strong sense of grace in the sermon. For me, I was overpowered by the effect of having spent time with Amos and of his influence upon me that week. Grace was not something I would have identified as a feature. That the congregation did identify it led me to marvel at the presence of Christ especially in the moment of sermon delivery. Somehow being incarnated in the text subsequently positions the preacher to witness the incarnation in their pastoral context. The words of Jesus to the first disciples speak of following the leading of the Spirit in bearing testimony to Christ: "When the Advocate comes, whom I will send to you from the Father, the Spirit of truth who comes from the Father, he will testify on my behalf. You also are to testify because you have been with me from the beginning" (John 15:26–27). *Lectio divina* and Ignatian Gospel Contemplation assist in attuning the preacher to this work of and with the Spirit.

Another effect of dwelling with the text through *lectio divina* and Ignatian Gospel Contemplation was to enable the preacher to gain an appreciation of the dimensions and landscape of the biblical world. It assisted in throwing into clearer relief the relationship between the Bible, the preacher and the world they inhabit today. Group members were given an article by Long[9] in which an incident involving a student of Long's was mentioned. After visiting Palestine the student was overwhelmed by the vast gulf between contemporary society and the historical context of the Bible. The student used to preach as if "Abraham and Sarah . . . were people who could have lived on my street . . . who could have been comfortable at worship in our church,"[10] but now the student did not know what to say about such biblical characters from the pulpit. The telling of this incident especially aided one participant in clarifying the dynamic she was experiencing during this process. The biblical

---

9. Thomas G. Long, "The Use of Scripture in Contemporary Preaching," *Interpretation* 44, no. 4 (1990): 341–352.

10. Long, "The Use of Scripture," 345.

world is so foreign but in the expediency of crafting a sermon this glaring fact can be quickly airbrushed in the effort to apply it to today. Both the biblical text and the preacher lose integrity in such a transaction. The priority for the person praying the Scripture might be to engage with this problem. Obvious exegetical concerns and mysteries emerge which must be contended with. However, a legitimate alternative starting point is how the text is moving the person praying this very same Scripture. To approach a passage in Genesis with the primary objective of seeking to somehow overlay the cultural setting of Abraham and Sarah on, for example, twenty-first-century New Zealand will result in one kind of sermon. To dwell with it, with the starting point being how it moves a preacher praying that passage, will result in quite another. Josie made the crucial point that the insights she receives from such a starting point form the backdrop to the sermon, "not necessarily what the people are going to get plonked in front of them." Such a backdrop then informs and earths the necessary exegetical work.

In chapter 2, discussion was given to the practice of reading Scripture aloud. Participants engaged in this practice during the *lectio* phase of *lectio divina* and the First Prelude of Ignatian Gospel Contemplation. The huge significance and impact of reading aloud was evident from the training day meeting until the final group meeting, when Frank essentially summed up everyone's experience: "The discovery I made about Scripture is quite a simple one but quite a profound one in my estimate, and that is by reading Scripture out loud, that has become quite a *huge insight* into the text." The consensus was that Scripture read aloud, in no small way, was a crucial element in locating the person in the text. If dwelling with the text was the desired place to be, then reading the passage aloud, at the very least, powerfully positioned the person at the gateway to such a place. Helen made the observation that reading aloud enriched the step into contemplation, whereas reading silently tended to make it a more cerebral exercise. The benefits of reading aloud included providing focus on the content of Scripture and minimizing mental distractions. It created a slower reading of the passage, which meant that otherwise familiar parts were not glossed over and new details were able to be noticed. For example, before I prayed the passage Mark 8:27 – 9:1 (Peter's declaration at Caesarea Philippi), I had thought that the first thing Jesus did after Peter rebuked him was to utter, "Get behind me, Satan!" (Mark 8:33). However, through the careful reading of this text I noted that the first thing he did was to turn and look at the other disciples. The observation of this pause in action lent itself to fruitful insight. Other benefits of reading

Scripture aloud included the varying of vocal expression during the reading, drawing the reader even more into the passage. The change in relationship between preacher and Scripture was predicated to a significant degree on this simple act. It resulted in reverent expectancy and enhanced the powers of concentration for the remaining time of prayer and dwelling in the text.

We have seen in this first cluster of themes that the initial sense of loss concerning the group's devotion to Christ and inattention to the mission to preach was replaced with a sense of refreshment and "fire in the belly." *Lectio divina* and Ignatian Gospel Contemplation re-orientated them to a renewed genesis of the person of the preacher and the messages they deliver. As participants prayed, they were gripped by the content and characters of the texts and found a new degree of confidence in their study and preaching. This confidence also translated to empowering their sense of discernment when weighing up alternative modes of preaching in our era. They discovered that they were more attentive and present to the Scriptures and consequently to their congregations. They found that reading Scripture aloud powerfully facilitated a keener sense of concentration on and observation of the message of the text. They rediscovered the power of abiding in Christ (John 15:1–10) and bearing fruit for him. While they had begun this research somewhat bewildered and saddened by their ministry experience, they also began this research serious about rekindling their first love for God and his mission, and found that by immersing themselves in his Word, through the agency of the two prayers, their lives were opened to his presence in fresh ways.

4

Repositioning

As the group engaged with the prayer disciplines at the initial retreat in November 2009, two main responses emerged. The first was unbridled enthusiasm at the immediate insights gained and their renewed connection with God and his Word as they employed *lectio divina* and Ignatian Gospel Contemplation. The second was concern whether this experience would or could be replicated in the cut and thrust of day-to-day pastoral ministry. Participants were acutely aware of the challenge that would confront them as they endeavoured to incorporate this kind of prayerful engagement with the Scriptures as part of regular sermon preparation. Michael, who was powerfully impacted by the effect of the prayers at the training day, commented, "But . . . how I'm going to pull it off in my normal life will be another challenge."

The proposed time commitment was not onerous as group members had been told that the rule of thumb was to pray for no less than fifteen minutes and usually about thirty minutes. Admittedly, the time allowed for participants to engage with the prayer at the retreat ranged from forty-five minutes to an hour, and this may have accentuated the sense that this would be unrealistic once back in pastoral ministry. The venue for the retreat was a Franciscan retreat centre, and this tranquil setting also accentuated the gulf between this particular day and their normal rhythm of ministry. After praying Psalm 84 using *lectio divina*, Helen reported that had she been in her normal context she would have automatically gravitated to the sections she knew well. This admission demonstrates how the rigours and pressures of pastoral ministry can drive preachers to approach the Scriptures with an expedient spirit rather than an exploratory one.

This chapter, then, explores the challenges and struggles created in the process of this research exercise. We will discuss two main themes that summarize the difficulties participants encountered: the impact of wider pastoral demands upon the time of sermon preparation, and the difficulty participants experienced in deciding which insights received during prayer were appropriate for public expression in the sermon. We will then examine two further themes which somewhat helped resolve these difficulties: the effect of the Third Prelude of Ignatian Gospel Contemplation and the utilization of exegesis.

The Effect of Time Pressure and Pastoral Demands

Accompanying the realization of the challenges ahead, which was reached at the retreat, was evidence that all seven group members were inspired to reposition themselves as preachers within their contexts upon their return. Helen spoke of the kaleidoscope of pressures and perceptions surrounding ministers today. Her survey ranged from parishioners remarking that they "cannot imagine what you do between Sundays" to the intimidating legacy of super-preachers who "are having endless quiet times as preachers and pondering and reflecting . . . And have got the luxury of [time for] endless word studies or whatever." She posited that either preachers are able to organize their ministries in such a way, or they are wedded to "the 'Word for the Day'[1] sermon preparation methodology *because* of the tyranny of trying to keep the church and its programmes going in this era." This aspect of workload and time pressure attested to by the group was a contributing factor to their perceived loss of connection with God and their struggle to retain vibrancy within their preaching ministries. However, the exposure to the prayer disciplines at the retreat and discussion around their use galvanized the group's resolve to exploit the opportunity this research offered. Gwen commented that the exercise in *lectio divina* had given her enough material for a year and that she was especially struck by the sense that "*we're* supposed to be God's dwelling place." She spoke further about her desire which had been intensified that year:

> I was very challenged earlier in the year by the verse "We preached and you believed" (1 Cor 15:11). And I thought if only I could preach so that people could believe . . . I do it a bit by the

---

1. The "Word for Today" is a popular daily devotional reading guide which includes a verse and an accompanying thought and/or story for each day. Within the context of the group discussion it was used as a euphemism for biblical illiteracy among congregations and the paucity of in-depth study and engagement with Scripture on the part of either the preacher or the congregation.

seat of my pants . . . some weeks it is much smoother than other weeks and this "We preached so that you believed" has been a challenge for me this year.

At this early stage of the process, the two prayer disciplines offered promise for such aspirations to be pursued and realized.

When the group convened for the second time the dominant reflection centred on the terrible onslaught of time and other pressures upon the time of prayer. Josie's summary accurately described everyone's experience: "I knew my days were interrupted but it wasn't until I started this process that I realized how much. How much I interrupt myself and how much I get external interruptions. And both weeks I had to split the contemplation time just because I wasn't able to get a peaceful hour. Which shocked me." As previously mentioned, such a battle had been predicted by the group, but its intensity had been underestimated. *Lectio divina* and Ignatian Gospel Contemplation offered a way of ministry which could clearly be seen but would not be able to be embraced without fundamental changes. Frank found that he gravitated towards the way he had studied in the past and, for no other reason than time and pressure, wrestled with stilling himself to attend to the process. He said, "This stuff takes time and I'm in a hurry . . . There's something saying 'The pressure's on, Frank. You're wasting time here. Get on to the real stuff.'" Given that all the group members were ministers of the gospel attempting to pray the Scriptures, the terrible irony of Frank's sentiment and its applicability was not lost on them. Michael lamented, "We are ordained to Word and sacrament by the PCANZ and that's pretty much the last thing we have time for during a busy week."[2] The agency of the two prayer disciplines revealed that the very pastoral context into which they are called to preach in fact conspires to derail their attempts to do so. This is not to suggest that there is a conspiracy on the part of the congregation, but rather that the whole (the resultant pastoral context) is greater than the sum of the parts (e.g. particular pastoral needs, weekly deadline for the sermon and worship preparation, funerals, community work and meetings).

The struggle with finding time to attend to the two prayer disciplines did not abate during the four-month research phase; however, group members marshalled new insights and convictions in response to it. Towards the end of

---

2. Michael was quoting the fundamental ordination vow and definition of a minister within the Presbyterian Church of Aotearoa New Zealand. While other denominations were represented in the group, his comment was relevant to all involved despite the specific reference to PCANZ.

the four months Helen reflected, "*I've* been challenged. Where does it begin? . . . For me I've been challenged to think the Scripture is the beginning . . . I've been reminded in a busy life to remember where the genesis is and how I go about discerning that for this week for this community."

In large measure, the battle to find time to attend to prayer both exposed the major reason why they had lost a noticeable degree of their first love for God and his Scriptures, and revealed why it was important to continue to fight for time. At the last meeting, Josie said, "I've had a taste of this [the effect of *lectio divina* and Ignatian Gospel Contemplation] and would like to become increasingly defiant in the face of all these other pressures." The pronounced experience of this struggle presented itself as a significant crossroads for the group members. The ongoing difficulty in setting aside time to pray had not only exposed why they had lost their first love; it also threatened to undermine the gains mentioned in chapter 3 insofar as an increase in authenticity and dwelling with the text were concerned. They were repositioned to respond to the call to seek Christ and his Word (2 Tim 2:15; 4:1–2), yet ironically their wider leadership responsibilities and concerns seemed to draw them away from this. Helen said, "I think that God-encounter bit in our preaching [preparation] is the bit in a busy week, with not a whole lot of volunteers to do the other jobs, . . . that suffers with our engagement with this [*lectio divina* and Ignatian Gospel Contemplation]." Despite their constant discussion and reflection during the four months they met with each other, they did not discover a particular strategy to combat this issue. While their awareness, convictions and appreciation of the problem were honed to a helpful degree, all seven participants were left, in one sense, feeling that they had not made any progress. At the final meeting Bob cited this aspect as the only disappointment he experienced in the whole process: the inability to devote the time to the prayer that he would have liked. Of all the issues which emerged during the research, this was the one which posed the greatest threat to the effectiveness of both prayer disciplines.

The Tension between Personal Devotions and Formal Sermon Preparation

Regarding issues which threatened the gains experienced through the utilization of the two prayer disciplines, only one other matched the above-mentioned problem in terms of significance. To the extent to which participants encountered God in the time of prayer they experienced a subsequent tension as how much of that encounter it was appropriate to include in the sermon. In short, most participants discovered that the prayer bore fruit but there was a reticence on their part for that to be translated to the sermon. It was as if their stated hope to reconnect with God devotionally had been fulfilled, only for it to threaten their accompanying hope to revive their first love for preaching. In chapter 3, various advances in the area of personal authenticity were described. These included growth in confidence as a preacher, in honesty before God and the text, and in subsequent sermon content which, while making the preacher vulnerable, proved powerful for the congregation. Initially this struggle was puzzling in the extreme. They had committed themselves to a time of conscious prayer for the purpose of sermon preparation. Why, then, was it proving so difficult for some to integrate the prayer into the sermon? The reticence appeared to be based on several overarching themes. These included a strongly held conviction that there must be a dichotomy between personal devotions and sermon preparation: either a concern that such an encounter with God was too personal to share or a lack of confidence on the part of the preacher that such fruit would be of any value to their congregation.

Throughout the research phase the emphasis was frequently made that they were first and foremost seeking God. This spiritual pursuit overshadowed all that they did and defined their sermon preparation; they were never just writing a sermon. As mentioned in chapter 3, at the retreat the group talked extensively about the traditional view, especially advocated during formal theological training, that sermon preparation ought never to double as a time of personal devotion. The subsequent discussion was revelatory for some group members as others spoke of how they derived spiritual nourishment from their sermon preparation. Frank referred to the Puritan preacher Richard Baxter, who observed, in Frank's words, "The preacher is of all people actually the most blessed, inasmuch as every day is the Sabbath . . . Every day you're doing the stuff which the congregation tends to focus on on Sunday. And you're in it all the time." Even though the discussion was not intended to come to a place of agreement, a discernible consensus was reached that this research exercise would facilitate the kind of prayer experience which nourishes the preacher and the congregation. However, the dichotomy between personal devotions and formal sermon preparation proved as strong as ever once the research phase commenced. The dichotomy re-emerged because of the nature of revelation received during the prayer and it led to another pervasive theme which stalled some group members.

The insights received from praying the Scriptures were variously described as too personal, too tough or, because of their specificity, peripheral to a more traditional reading of the text.

A fair generalization is that once in prayer, group members were so caught up in the experience that the notion of sermon writing was forgotten for the moment. For instance, at the February group meeting Bob said, "I just found myself getting into [the Scripture] and quite enjoying it and thinking 'Oh *bother*. I actually have to write a sermon. This is fun.'" Later in April, he was still encountering this issue, commenting, "I've found engaging with these disciplines very helpful and, in fact, almost got to that stage . . . where I thought, 'Man, this is *great*. [But] now I've got to go and *preach it*.'" Kathy reinforced this by saying, "The thought of writing a sermon was actually a distraction . . . When I go into it, thinking I've to write a sermon out of this, it destroys the process." Gwen described encountering a gap between the moment of prayer and the sermon. During the research phase she played with several metaphors, such as "tunnel," "bridge" and "funnel," to describe the gulf between the two and how to make the transition. She did not settle on any which really captured what proved to be a deep frustration for her. Interestingly, Gwen was the one who initially suggested that there ought not to be a dichotomy between personal devotions and sermon preparation. However, the experience of *lectio divina* and Ignatian Gospel Contemplation appeared to create such a separation for her. On one occasion she spoke of her annoyance with the text: "It was speaking more to me about things I didn't want to speak to the congregation about." However, Michael's experience was especially pronounced:

> I got to this extreme high where I was really talking to Jesus like I never have before. It was just amazing. But it was so amazingly high . . . in this personal time that when it came to prepare the sermon it was the worst low. *Like, is this bi-polar preaching?* The heights of high, and then converting the peace and what I found through the Ignatian Contemplation into the sermon was the pits. It was the worst.

The prayer regularly arrested the participants to the point that it mysteriously proved, at least initially, counter-productive. This conundrum was intensified because both prayer disciplines, especially Ignatian Gospel Contemplation, are predicated on action subsequent to the prayer. In chapter 2, Brou's contention concerning post-contemplation action and preaching was cited: "For even as it is better to enlighten than merely shine, so it is better to give to others the fruits of one's contemplation than merely to contemplate."[3] Admittedly, not all post-contemplation action would necessarily warrant a sermon, but the depth of struggle which threatened to result in no sermon at all seemed anathema to the spirit of both prayer disciplines.

This issue not only threatened to undermine advances in personal authenticity insofar as honesty and confidence were concerned, it also fought against the advances of increased discernment described in chapter 3. At times, group members received insights which they deemed too specific and unconventional to be given major expression, if any at all, in their sermons. During one group meeting this issue was particularly prominent. Helen had previously discussed how the prayer disciplines had enabled her to locate her "sermon in a sentence." Her experience was that the effect of the prayer equipped her to craft the sermon proposition or the main theme which would drive the sermon. However, Kathy stated that she had been thinking extensively about Helen's comment and had hoped that she too could locate her sermons in a sentence, but that it had not proven to be the case.[4] She continued with the observation: "I, as the participant in the process, won't always come up with what is suitable for the proposition for the sermon. For instance, just this morning I [prayed Daniel 1] . . . And what I personally linked into will not be what I bring out as the theme." Kathy explained that while engaging with the narrative in Daniel 1 she was struck by the description in verse 2 of the fate of the vessels from the temple in Jerusalem.[5] She described the moment of encounter:

> It *really* hit me the *disappointment* that God must have felt with the vessels going in this place. I actually came out with four points that really attracted me . . . [but] that hit me more than the rest. The *disappointment*. And yet I . . . still think the theme of this passage is about them standing up for what is right.

---

3. Brou, *Ignatian Methods of Prayer*, 28.

4. While Kathy was the most inexperienced preacher in the group, this was offset by her postgraduate study at Masters level and significant experience in the field of education, which impacted the way she structured and developed her sermons. Hence the following sequence of events cannot be attributed to lack of experience as it also in large measure centred on exegetical and hermeneutical considerations with which Kathy was au fait.

5. "The Lord let King Jehoiakim of Judah fall into his [Nebuchadnezzar's] power, as well as some of the vessels of the house of God. These he brought to the land of Shinar, and placed the vessels in the treasury of his gods" (Dan 1:2).

Kathy proceeded to explain that the main thrust of her message would centre on Daniel and his colleagues refusing to eat and drink the royal rations. The disappointment of God might be a main point or an illustration but not the sermon proposition and theme. The resultant group discussion was marked by high energy and a deep sense of wonder as group members were equally struck by Kathy's revelation. She was given strong encouragement to pursue the disappointment of God as the main theme. The other group members present, including myself, agreed that they had all heard the kind of sermon from Daniel 1 about doing the right thing, but none of the group had considered it from the perspective of God's disappointment. In fact, even in the very moment of discussing this feature of God's disappointment, it bore immediate fruit. Gwen later spoke of how when Kathy described this theme she had felt sadness and it prompted her to consider her own life and ministry. This incident, centred on material from Daniel 1, powerfully illustrated the difficult decisions the participants were confronted with in making the transition from prayer to formal sermon preparation. It also demonstrates that while the preacher might glean an insight, courage in exercising discernment to utilize such material in the sermon proposition is called for. Exegetical concerns remain an important consideration in the process, as such insights still need to be tested. It does not always follow that a significant insight received in prayer automatically reflects the sense of the text. The potential to do violence to the text by advancing a personal insight as the main theme, instead of allowing it to add a hue to the sermon, remains. The place of exegesis will be discussed later in this chapter.

The intensity with which some in the group struggled with these issues was unexpected. Yet four participants regularly encountered this issue to a marked degree. I had expected that all the group members would subscribe to the kind of ethos expressed by Frank: "I approach it (*lectio divina* and Ignatian Gospel Contemplation) as I am here as a preacher. And I'm in community with the congregation, therefore, 'What is it saying to us?'" I echoed Frank's sentiments to the group with the comment, "We're doing this with preaching in mind . . . There's nothing wrong with us being the first person to be touched by the message so that we can embody it and preach it."

The *raison d'être* of a preacher is to bring the Scriptures to bear upon the church of Christ as she worships and obeys him in the time and culture in which her members live. The church sets aside men and women whom they recognize as gifted and called to study, pray and present the Scriptures to the people of God. The church therefore holds the reasonable expectation that when their minister or pastor stands before them to preach, they do so having prayerfully studied the Scriptures. While every group member would agree to this, it seemed a contradiction in terms that in the very act of preparing for a sermon the preacher would conceal the fruit gained through praying for the sermon. Helen began to touch on some of the reasons for the struggle. The preacher is subject to the very forces of the culture of the day into which they are ministering. Insofar as part of the culture is frenetic busyness and a reduction in time afforded by volunteers, the preacher's primary call to spend time with God and the Scriptures is crowded out instead of their defying such pressures upon their time. The cost the preacher pays is to revert to preparing sermons by going, as Helen put it, "into autopilot." Not only is the preacher's effectiveness as a preacher eroded by this, but so is their opportunity to model to the congregation spirituality marked by time spent with God.

In chapter 1 we considered how *lectio divina* and Ignatian Gospel Contemplation were, to an extent, shaped by the culture of their day and yet transcended it. *Lectio divina* paid dues to the emergence of reason in the period of scholasticism but also breathed life into a spiritual climate bereft of theological reflection and mystery. In the sixteenth century, Ignatian Gospel Contemplation broadened the emphasis on doctrine and the mystical to include the use of emotion and imagination. Ignatius facilitated a shift from a super-spiritual approach to the mystical body of Christ to an appreciation of and pragmatic interaction with the humanity of Jesus. Brackley[6] and Rahner[7] spoke of Ignatius and his work as a product of his times and reaching beyond them.

We also considered Rahner's prediction that Ignatian spirituality transcended the modern era and was a sign of the approaching future, a time we are surely in the midst of. *Lectio divina* and Ignatian Gospel Contemplation have proved to be historically and culturally relevant and prophetic to that same historical and cultural context. Against this backdrop, it is salutary to consider the group's struggle and subsequent example and discussion of contemporary cultural and spirit-of-the-age considerations as they pertain to the use of both prayer disciplines. My contention is that one of the reasons the struggle proved so intense is due to the peculiarities of New Zealand, or to use its colloquial name, Kiwi, culture.[8] To an extent,

---

6. Brackley, *Call to Discernment.*

7. Rahner, *Spirituality of the Church.*

8. All group members are NZ-born.

the innate cultural norms usurped the newly learned and experienced value of the prayer disciplines. *Lectio divina* and Ignatian Gospel Contemplation facilitate the otherness of the gospel over and against the spirit of the age. They have the potential to position the person in a new place from which to articulate the message of Scripture with a prophetic edge. In my view, in the aftermath of prayer, some group members critiqued whether particular prayerful insights were appropriate yet left cultural habits unexamined. Kiwi culture obviously flavours New Zealand church life and definitely colours the ministry of preaching. I believe the nature of Kiwi preaching, as it reflects Kiwi culture, was at play in the reticence to utilize what seemed to be fitting material for the sermon.

This realization confronted me and necessitated reflection on the contours of Kiwi culture in the pulpit. Such an exercise is incumbent upon all preachers in all cultures. Questions surrounding Christ, culture and church must be engaged with so as to better discern what the Spirit is saying to the church in any age in any continent and country. Our point of reference and example is the way the ascended and glorified Christ addresses issues in the seven churches of Asia Minor (Rev 2–3) by constantly using points of cultural connection. The message of Christ to the seven churches is couched in the cultural language of the cities each of the churches existed in. Both commendation and correction were given cultural context so as to better appeal to the sensibilities of the people of God. It makes for insightful and incisive reading as both comforting and disturbing words are delivered. It is important for preachers the world over to reflect on their cultural context, asking how it enhances or hinders a response to Christ and his work. It was this kind of pressure and realization that necessitated the following reflection on the New Zealand context.

The cultural qualities demonstrated by Kiwi preachers have been described by the mnemonic LUCIS:[9]

---

9. Paul Windsor, "Introduction to Preaching," course taught at Carey Baptist College, Auckland, 2005.

Paul Windsor developed this mnemonic upon returning to NZ in the late 1980s after extensive time in India as a "missionary kid" and under-/postgraduate theological study in the US. His particular forte is in the area of preaching and his twenty years as a lecturer and principal in NZ theological colleges have been marked by an emphasis in training preachers. He was initially puzzled as to why the most effective NZ preachers were markedly different from more prominent US and British preachers. The mnemonic LUCIS summarizes his observations. Further, he observes that, while the careful use of words and oratory is valued in US, British and even Indian contexts, this is not so much the case in NZ. He cites an article written about the NZ Prime Minister David Lange (PM 1984–1989), which indicted that

- Laidback
- Understated
- Conversational
- Informal
- Self-deprecating

These five characteristics are weighted towards the moment of sermon delivery and identify the kind of preaching which connects with New Zealanders. Nevertheless, the features of LUCIS are not divorced from the backstage work for the sermon's final form and delivery. Of these five characteristics, it appears that the tendencies of Kiwi preachers to be understated, informal and self-deprecating were contributing cultural factors to the research outcomes experienced by the research participants. Being understated translated into a reluctance to include material which could be construed as being above their station and to suffering the fate of prophets in their own country. Being informal dictated that if the material was to be used it would need to be toned down so as not to be too heavy or intense. Being self-deprecating meant that any sharing of the material would be instinctively turned back on the preacher so as to honour the treasured cultural norm of egalitarianism.

The most powerful New Zealand cultural traits at play can be distilled down and reworded as modesty and restraint.[10] These two particular cultural traits appeared to be the source of difficulty experienced by group members in articulating material discovered during their prayer. Bold sermon content would clash with the cultural norm to be humble, understated and self-effacing. The cultural feature of restraint holds the negative trait of over-caution, which was evident as the group discussed their decision-making process concerning sermon content emerging from their time of prayer.

While specific New Zealand cultural issues were not discussed as a group, on several occasions the group did discuss the effect of personality types upon the use of the prayer disciplines. Such discussion centred mostly,

---

one reason he did not last as PM was because he used words too well. Lange's oratory skills bred distrust and suspicion among constituents because they were unsure if what he was saying was really what was meant. Windsor states that when he discusses this mnemonic in preaching classes it has a polarizing effect. He comments that Pentecostals and ethnic churches, such as Chinese and Samoan, still desire to see something of the orator in the pulpit. The influence of television preachers appears to shape expectations as well. Also, NZ Pentecostals tend to especially model their ministries on US examples. Windsor adds that the view that emerges in most discussions on LUCIS is that because of the influence of Pentecostalism and the growth of ethnic churches in NZ, there is a sense that there may be a breakdown of the LUCIS reality.

10. Cathrin Schaer, "She's Right, Mate," *Canvas* (2006): 11.

but not solely, on Myers-Briggs type-indicators (MBTI) and to some measure began to point towards social and cultural influences in their preaching. Those group members who were proficient in understanding their own MBTI profile used it as a reference point for their own reflection. It was the consensus of the group, based on this research exercise, that regardless of personality type all ought to engage with the prayers. They considered that once engaged with the prayer disciplines the particular personality type would then direct where it led or whether, to quote Helen, "it becomes the air they breathe." Interestingly, the group's answer to the question "Would you recommend these prayer disciplines to all personality types or would you have conditions?" was that people should commit to them and persist. Helen provided a representative statement of the group's finding: "Go beyond yourself. Don't give into yourself too quickly because this [*lectio divina* and Ignatian Gospel Contemplation] is important." The reflection on personality types sits with the discussion of cultural aspects but the lack of reflection upon their own cultural expression was a blind spot. Given the integrity with which the group wrestled with aspects of their personality preferences, I am confident that if cultural categories had been aired, their response would have been similar.

Given that the discussion of personality types resulted in an endorsement of *lectio divina* and Ignatian Gospel Contemplation for different personalities, I believe that, with time, they would have endorsed the same with reference to historical and cultural forces. As principal researcher in the exercise I take responsibility for not having identified the cultural aspects sooner and facilitated group discussion accordingly. However, during the analysis of the field data and my reflection on Kiwi culture and its effect on this exercise, I emailed cultural reflections to group members for their response. I suggested that issues of modesty and restraint may have influenced their decision whether to include insights from the prayer in the sermon. Of the seven group members, six were in a position to respond to the email. While essentially the responses constituted a straw poll without the advantages of face-to-face discussion, four group members endorsed the observation and two disagreed. However, insofar as both prayer disciplines have been historically proven to enable Christians to engage with and rise above their cultural contexts, it is exciting to consider that they experienced the beginnings of that. This was even though they had just fallen short of being able to articulate and identify that aspect precisely during the research phase. In her response, Josie pointed out, "I would think that this process helped me feel more confident that I had something to offer given the Kiwi context of modesty and restraint." Furthermore, this confidence was largely based on the nature of the content and insights facilitated by the two prayer disciplines. Hence, in a culture where it is frowned upon to hold oneself up as an example, there were the beginnings of a new way by which preachers were able to express leadership and present a call to their congregations to "Be imitators of me, as I am of Christ" (1 Cor 11:1).

The Value of the Ignatian Gospel Contemplation's Third Prelude

Indeed, while the struggle was intense in deciding if insights gained during the prayer were to be preached, it did not eventuate that these insights were never aired. The struggle in making the transition from prayer to sermon preparation was eased, in some measure, from an unexpected quarter. Initially group members struggled with comprehending and exercising the Third Prelude of Ignatian Gospel Contemplation. The Third Prelude is the point in the prayer where the desired grace is prayed for (see chapter 2). Yet while this aspect of Ignatian Gospel Contemplation initially caused the most consternation within the group, it eventually proved to be the part of the prayer which resulted in the most fruit. It took two to four times using Ignatian Gospel Contemplation before it seemed to resonate with participants. Josie remarked, "My first experience of that particular discipline I struggled with . . . The next time it just really clicked. And I think it is just something that takes a bit of practice and experience." Michael had initially struggled with connecting with Ignatian prayer at all and the difficulty was exacerbated by time pressures. Within this context, the Third Prelude emerged as the redeeming and defining feature. "But I must say . . . that even with the struggling with the Ignatian [prayer] and the time, the great thing about it, I found the grace in it. When you're asking for the graces." Kathy also initially failed to grasp the concept of the Third Prelude, but by the second group meeting stated it was now "one of the most significant parts of [the Ignatian prayer] now that I understand it." Once the group settled into the rhythm of the Third Prelude, its effect became evident, especially for three group members. It proved to be the unifying feature between the time of prayer and the subsequent sermon content.

It appears that the praying for and outworking of the Third Prelude transcended any perceived evaluation of the success or failure of how the prayer time was construed. Michael spoke of how even when the sermon preparation had not gone well, he found that praying for the desired grace crystallized any disparate elements. He said, "[Regardless of] how good, bad or indifferent the sermon [was, I would pray], 'Lord, that's where you're getting the job done.'" Kathy described how the use of the Third Prelude had evolved in her sermon preparation and made the transition to her congregation:

> I found the grace the most powerful thing . . . in terms of the sermon as well that seems to be what I am asking for in response to this passage. When you do a sermon you want people to respond in some way and it is the grace where it is at for me. What are you asking of me in this passage? What are you asking of me when I read this text? How can I interact with it personally? And that's how I use the grace.

After the end of the formal research phase, Kathy emailed an unsolicited comment about the Third Prelude: "I have found the 'grace' in Ignatian Contemplation much easier to translate into a [sermon] proposition – it's a classic, concise set-up!" It would appear that in the experience of the group, it was in this particular element of the prayer that the movement of the Spirit was clearly evident. Hence, the perceived presence and work of the Spirit provided the confidence, courage and conviction to now make the prayer content sermon content. At the last group meeting, participants were invited to complete the sentence "In the light of this experience, it seems good to the Holy Spirit and us . . ."[11] Josie finished the sentence with: " that for all the initial weirdness and difficulty in understanding how to utilize the Ignatian Gospel Contemplation's Third Prelude of asking for and desiring grace, this is the part of the prayer that is the most powerful." Insofar as participants received an answer to their prayer for the desired grace, they subsequently felt inspired and compelled to make that the major unifying theme and call in their sermon. While the group did not discuss whether there was a corresponding feature in *lectio divina*, I would identify *oratio* as the nearest element to the Third Prelude. While the word or phrase identified during *lectio* did not always translate as the main driver for the sermon, such a theme would emerge in the later stages of *lectio divina* as the initial point of identification was processed. From my experience, it was during the time of response and *oratio* that such a theme would be clarified and the movement

---

11. This phrase is adopted from Acts 15:28 (the Council of Jerusalem). The sense of divine and human collaboration captured the experimental sense of this research and facilitated good reflection of the process.

of the Spirit consolidated. It was the effect of *oratio* which would generate "fire in the belly" and provide a surge of energy to begin to formulate the sermon.

The Place of Exegesis

In terms of its importance for preaching, the historical-critical exegetical method has rightly assumed a place of prominence. It does need to be acknowledged that the definition of the "historical-critical method" is somewhat fluid and that it "may be more appropriate to speak of 'historical-critical methods' (plural) rather than of 'the historical-critical method' (singular)."[12] The focus of this work assumes the continued influence of the historical-critical method upon week-by-week preaching. As a discipline, this method works to ensure that the preacher studies the text with integrity. Yet it is not without its problems:

> The constraints of the historical-critical method of biblical criticism and its collusion with modernity inhibit a participative reading of Scripture and a wider, fertile way of knowing. While this methodology has enormous value in considering the historical situation of the text, it violates the nature of the text it is interpreting.[13]

By its very nature, Scripture endeavours to evoke total participation from the reader.[14] However, because the historical-critical method did not emerge from the Reformation but from the Enlightenment, its view of history is one of cause and effect and, as such, presupposes a closed universe which does not easily accommodate the dynamism of Scripture.[15] "Historically, the historical-critical method came from the outside and did not arise from the very nature of faith."[16] All seven participants were trained exegetes and took

---

12. Sidney Greidanus, *The Modern Preacher and the Ancient Text: Interpreting and Preaching Biblical Literature* (Grand Rapids: Eerdmans, 1988), 25.

13. Laurel Gasque, "The Bible of the Poor: An Example of Medieval Interpretation and Its Relevance Today," in *Imagination and Interpretation: Christian Perspectives*, ed. Hans Boersma (Vancouver: Regent College, 2005), 66.

14. Eugene H. Peterson, *Reversed Thunder: The Revelation of John and the Praying Imagination* (San Francisco: HarperSanFrancisco, 1988).

15. George E. Ladd, "The Search for Perspective," *Interpretation* 25, no. 1 (1971); Greidanus, *The Modern Preacher*; William W. Klein, Craig L. Blomberg and Robert L. Hubbard Jr., *Introduction to Biblical Interpretation*, 2nd ed. (Nashville: Thomas Nelson, 2004); Gasque, "The Bible of the Poor."

16. Ladd, "The Search for Perspective," 49.

seriously the importance of studying the text in sound and conventional ways. Yet, prior to their involvement in this exercise, they attested to the dangers and difficulties when regularly handling Scripture, as outlined in chapter 1. The main hazard was finding oneself regularly unmoved and untouched by the very Scriptures being studied for the sermon. We saw a corrective to this in chapter 3 with the experience of group members recovering their first love for God and their passion for preaching. However, the benefits of remaining committed to sound exegetical practices in concert with the prayers were also experienced. While the Third Prelude helped to relieve the tension in making the transition from prayer to sermon content, traditional exegetical methods also proved a helpful partner in the process. However, the timing of employing exegesis proved to be crucial.

All the group members, without exception, discovered that the best time to perform exegesis was after the text had been prayed using one of the two prayer disciplines. Not surprisingly, the consensus was that to consult commentaries as a first step would unduly influence the subsequent reading and prayer of the primary text. Participants favoured engaging with the text before any thought was given to theme, sermon structure or work with the original language or context. When difficulty was struck during the prayer and a passage proved too difficult to reasonably proceed, then secondary sources were consulted to aid the participant. Josie described one such occurrence while using *lectio divina* for a passage from 1 Corinthians:

> I was halfway through *lectio divina* and thought, "This is going to be a disaster." It was helpful [to consult a commentary] because it got me to grips with the text and it made me realize I can't pull a sermon from what I'm getting from the text. Spirit or not, I need to go and do some reading before I take this any further.

From my own experience, when praying in the book of Amos I found that an orientation to introductory material concerning the political and spiritual climate of the day was appropriate as a pre-prayer step. However, to have delved into verse-by-verse study and commentary would have been counter-productive. Yet even this occurrence was relatively rare in the group's experience. Throughout the four months of the research phase, it was found that participants instinctively and intentionally suspended their exegetical work until post-prayer. This development in the group members' sermon-preparation regime attests to the two levels of engagement with Scripture discussed in chapter 1 but also provides an adaptation of it. In chapter 1, attention was given to Merton's exhortation[17] that the first level, exegetical work, lead to a second level, deeper and personal engagement with the text. Merton, quoting Bultmann, posited that the first level is preparation for the second level. The group's experience attested to the powerful effect when the two levels enjoy an organic relationship; however, contrary to Merton's prescription, all seven members found attending to the second level before the first level more conducive to a deep and personal engagement with the text. In addition, to imply that the first and second levels are self-contained and clear categories is somewhat artificial. While there were obvious separate phases of prayer and exegetical work, there was an undercurrent of interplay between both throughout the time of sermon preparation. Regardless of how familiar or uncertain they were with a particular text, participants arrived at the time of prayer with exegetical instincts. Conversely, during the time of more academic exegetical work, the spirit of prayer was still guiding and informing their work. This latter point will be discussed further in chapter 5, when the findings relating to the concept of *contemplatives in action* will be highlighted.

Once prayer was completed, the place of exegesis was found not to be in violent opposition to the fruit gained from the prayer. Indeed, the group found their exegetical training comforting and referred to it positively in terms of law enforcement. Helen commented, "I think it [exegesis] becomes a bit like the police. It becomes like the monitor along the way when you take forays into other methods. It reminds you if you are veering off into *completely* subjective nothingness." Kathy claimed that she would never attempt the prayer disciplines without the accompanying discipline of exegesis and spoke of the organic relationship between the two: "It [*lectio divina* and Ignatian Gospel Contemplation] actually uncovers the questions I would ask in the remaining preparation time." They testified to an increased sense of confidence in dealing with the text as a result of the prayer, and the sense of safety, knowing that their insights would be further subject to historical, critical and grammatical exegetical study. As Josie described it, there are "two wings to the process, because you wouldn't ever want to just pursue your own confident path without having the double check of your [exegetical] process."

Boersma identified the loss for those who rely solely on the historical-critical method, remarking, "The need for the charisma of spiritual insight remains a riddle to those who restrict themselves to a purely historical

---

17. Merton, *Opening the Bible.*

interpretation and to an authorial intent found by means of 'objective' criteria."[18] Group members came to this research exercise as preachers who were weighted towards preparing sermons by relying on historical interpretation and authorial intent but were hungering for more. The recognition of the need for the charisma of spiritual insight was not a riddle for them, but possibly how to attain it was. As they prayed and experienced this charisma, the value of the historical-critical method was also experienced and the sum was greater than the parts. At the last group meeting it was remarked that, in one group member's experience, it was a pity that the prayer disciplines had not been part of preaching training along with exegesis and hermeneutics. Along with the Third Prelude, post-prayer exegetical work helped relieve the angst of what to now include in the sermon content.

Before leaving this discussion on exegesis, comment on one other aspect is necessary. When the group reflected on the tension concerning what from the prayer time it was appropriate to include in the sermon, it was not uncommon for them to speak of their unease that their insights might be nothing more than eisegesis. Eisegesis is the practice of reading things into the text, imposing presuppositions upon it and making it say something which is at odds with its intent. Michael remarked, "I'm thinking, what's prophetic, and what's me, and what's eisegesis?" Within the context of this research, the term "eisegesis" tended to be used in an over-scrupulous manner as group members endeavoured to work through how best to deal with insights received during their prayer. Interestingly, when eisegesis was spoken about, it was usually a signal that a group member had genuinely encountered God and the text and was now wrestling with how best to process that in the sermon. As a group they had begun to discover a type of eisegesis which can enrich preaching rather than represent all that is wrong with bad preaching. In their preparation, preachers contend with an awkward secret: eisegesis is needed when attempting exegesis. In the moment of study and application there is interplay between sound exegesis, hermeneutics, pressing contemporary issues, spiritual encounter, imagination and the spirit of the age. "The boldest way to put this is that a certain kind of *eisegesis*, the kind that renders us completely present before the text and passionately concerned to hear a Word that addresses our world, is not a sin to be avoided, but rather is an earnestly

---

18. Hans Boersma, "Spiritual Imagination: Recapitulation as an Interpretative Principle," in *Imagination and Interpretation: Christian Perspectives*, ed. Hans Boersma (Vancouver: Regent College, 2005), 31.

sought prerequisite to productive *exegesis*."[19] Nichols[20] makes a case for the Bible's robustness in being able to hold its own in a conversation with a reader who approaches with ideas and even answers. This presumes that the reader is aware of their human limitations and is committed to responding honestly and openly to the arguments the Bible presents in response. Nichols states:

> In fact, the bottom line of this talk about "eisegesis" probably has to be that there is no power on earth that could stop us from "reading into" a text no matter how piously we thought we were preparing its otherness – not, at least, if our understanding of processes of human perception or communication is even remotely accurate.[21]

In chapter 1, features of pre-modern, modern and post-modern interpretation of Scripture were summarized. Goldingay[22] suggests that now is the time to take the best of these three broad eras and synthesize their strengths. In the midst of their experience as research participants, the group may have prematurely dismissed as eisegesis a dynamic which actually was the beginning of such a synergy. While they endorsed intensely praying with the text prior to conducting historical-critical study, the unseen cost of that was a niggling and unfounded insecurity that they were subsequently guilty of eisegesis. Insofar as participants now had a first-hand contemporary experience with the text and then would contrast and compare that with the experience of the original author and audience through exegesis, yes, they had engaged in a form of eisegesis. There was no evidence that any participant acted irresponsibly in that process, but rather there was evidence that it was the kind of eisegesis which deserves rehabilitation in preaching ministries.

In this second cluster of themes we have considered four specific issues. Two of them – finding uninterrupted time to attend to prayer and wrestling with the decision of which insights from the prayer were appropriate for the sermon –represented significant struggles for group members; the other two issues – the Third Prelude of Ignatian Gospel Contemplation and the place of exegesis in the overall process – proved to be illuminating and helpful. We saw the

---

19. Long, "The Use of Scripture," 349, emphasis in original.
20. J. Randall Nichols, *Building the Word: The Dynamics of Communication and Preaching* (San Francisco: Harper & Row, 1980).
21. Ibid., 28.
22. Goldingay, "Pre-Modern, Modern and Post-Modern," 19.

effect upon the preacher who is assaulted by relentless pastoral demands and responsibilities other than attention to prayer and the study of the Scriptures. We saw too that participants demonstrated a heart receptive to the movement of the Spirit when praying the Scriptures with *lectio divina* and Ignatian Gospel Contemplation. There the preacher was confronted with new and personal revelations which caused further struggle as their appropriateness for public expression was weighed. Cultural background and context exacerbated this wrestling especially as it related to the Kiwi cultural norms of modesty and restraint. However, these constraints were alleviated by the experience of grace by virtue of the Third Prelude of Ignatian Gospel Contemplation. The revelation of grace emerged as a driver for the subsequent sermon and the key themes marshalled around it. Furthermore, sound attention to conventional exegetical methods post-prayer, whereby insights were tested against accepted scholarship, proved helpful in disempowering the struggles. This in turn was marked by an aversion, if not over-scrupulousness, regarding any perceived notion of eisegesis. Yet participants began to experience a kind of eisegesis which does not do violence to the text but aids in the experience of its message. Even so, participants subsequently found themselves occupying a new ministry space before their congregations, God and the world. It is to this last cluster of themes that we now turn.

5

Reorientation

In chapter 3, the initial reasons for group members agreeing to be a part of this research were described along with their hopes for the process. These included recovering from a perceived loss in their relationship with God and reviving their passion for preaching. Their felt sense of loss in their relationship with God and attention to preaching was intensified and defined by the weight of responsibility to faithfully minister to the people of God. Consequently, any hoped-for gains would be not just for the personal edification of the preacher but also for the benefit of the people they served. There was a beautiful symmetry in the group's intent to love God and serve him and to love the people they were called to minister to. Michael's comment at the training day illustrated this; he said he saw this research as "building into my life and building into my parish ministry and the church." Helen augmented this by identifying a common theme from the group discussion: how were their congregations relating to the Scriptures, and were they as preachers omitting anything in their ministries which hindered their congregations' connection with the Scriptures? Kathy summarized the group's discussion at the training day concerning their shared task: "You know, no matter how many techniques you have, it's that connecting with people – the struggle to make this connection." This desire was a strong unifying feature for the group from the outset of the research and its fulfilment a consistent source of encouragement during it. In chapter 3 we outlined the increase in the preacher's sense of authenticity. A strong facet of that authenticity translated to a new sense of connection with the congregation. To varying degrees, new and fresh connections with the congregation were experienced by all seven members of the group. In this chapter we will discuss the new forms of connection with the congregation that arose from this research, along with the power of the imagination and the wider effect of the two prayer disciplines experienced beyond sermon preparation.

New Connections with the Congregation

One of the evidences of a new sense of connection with the congregation was expressed in terms of precision when preaching to them. While all participants experienced this to one degree or another, four noted such precision particularly. The sermon content contained a new sense of relevance and distinctiveness that was applicable to one congregation but not necessarily to another. For instance, on Easter Sunday, two group members each focused on "dawn" for their sermon. One participant developed the theme that dawn represented a slow and emerging understanding that the resurrection had occurred. Yet it was marked by uncertainty and caution as the main players slowly emerged from the dark of night into the emerging light and pieced the events together. This sense flavoured the whole Sunday service, not just the sermon. A second group member had independently taken up the theme of dawn and for her context celebrated the new day dawning for Peter and all of humanity. In contrast to the other group member's use of dawn, this group member applied it in a more immediate and celebratory fashion. As they compared their material, the exactitude for their contexts was evident and the value for each congregation obvious. A bland and broad application of the text was replaced by a sense of relevance and immediacy. An attentiveness to the text through the prayer translated to an attentiveness to a particular congregation and the Word of God was experienced in a new way.

To the extent that a resolution was found for the struggle in deciding which insights gained during prayer were to be included in the sermon (see chapter 4), participants described a powerful movement from their individual experience to community involvement. Josie described the transition from her own encounter during prayer to the writing and delivery of the sermon in this way: "It is to some extent 'me, me, me', but from that foundation I've gone on to construct a sermon that's 'us, us, us.'" Bob discovered, "I think you're getting to the heart of not only what God wants to say to me as the person dealing with the text but what God could want to say to the people as well." Group members and their respective congregations appeared to enjoy a new sense of commonality as preacher and congregation engaged with the Word of God and they listened with rapt attention as it spoke with a new sense of urgency and particularity. Bob described how the prayer disciplines facilitated, on the one hand, a new awareness of the variety of listeners he preached to, and, on the other hand, a community response. Describing the effect of preaching on the Prodigal Son, he said, "It suddenly felt like we [the congregation] were tapping into how people felt." Just as authentic contemplation ought to lead to an increase in grace and commitment to Christ, so it should lead to greater unity and witness within and of the church. Scripture, the church and Christ are inseparable, and this vibrant relationship can be illustrated by an image spoken of by the church fathers:

> Mary, the mother of the Lord . . . was the receiver of God's word *par excellence*. She welcomed the Word in her mind before the Word became flesh in her body. In those secret months of cherishing and nurturing the Word, she became the model of the contemplative Church. Her words at the Annunciation might well be ours as we begin our *lectio*: "Behold the Lord's servant; let it be done to me according to your word" (Luke 1:38).[1]

To the extent that new connections were experienced with the congregation, they in fact became partners in the prayer initially prayed by the preacher and became impregnated with the Word. Nouwen,[2] expounding Luke 6:12–19, describes the pattern of Jesus' ministry as, first, praying and hearing from the Father; second, gathering a community in the aftermath of the prayer; and, third, ministering together. It was Nouwen's contention that the order can be erroneously reversed in that a failed attempt to minister is made, then an unsuccessful appeal to the community for help is expressed, and only then is prayer turned to as a last resort. The two prayer disciplines orientated group members to the pattern of Jesus' ministry so that they were able to experience a movement from individual prayer through to community unity and response predicated on a collective engagement with Scripture.

The mechanics of how the connection with the congregation developed was varied and not always easy to identify; however, one common denominator did emerge. On occasions, several of the preachers expressed that they had been so energized and caught up in the prayer that they could not contain or camouflage the experience when they preached. They felt compelled to somehow involve their congregations and call the people to the burden of the text and the revelation they had discerned. The most common

---

1. Casey, *Sacred Reading*, 43.
2. Henri Nouwen, "Moving from Solitude to Community to Ministry," *Leadership* (Spring 1995): 81–87.

way participants did this was by essentially revisiting the prayer experience during the sermon and, in doing so, inviting the congregation to join them. Michael, having contemplated a gospel event, had been so gripped by the radical nature of Jesus' words that

> I couldn't do anything but invite these people: "Look, let's join the crowd today. You've got to come in, and may you hear the words of Jesus. I want to hear. Please imagine you're in this large multitude who are listening to him . . . Let's join the crowd now and listen to him." I really wanted them to be there because of the radical nature of what Jesus was saying and re-saying to me.

Kathy had a similar experience. During a sermon, "I actually told them [the congregation] what I had done [in the prayer], and you could see them talking about their responses in the same way." Helen also overtly described the events of her prayer and in turn drew her congregation into the gospel scene. Reflecting on the outcome, she commented, "It was wonderful." The experience is tantamount to Jeremiah's (Jer 20:9), in which the Word is like fire in the bones and there is no option other than to tell it as it is. The interesting aspect of this finding is that it was utterly unanticipated. Group members had not been coached to do this nor been discouraged against such a practice. It simply emerged in each independently of the others, and yet collectively. Several of the participants initially questioned whether they ought to divulge such inner workings of their prayer time but reasoned that it was the most appropriate approach. Michael said of the compulsion he experienced, "I'm really desiring, when I'm reading the Scripture, to draw people into it. Or when you're preaching it or building up a scene – you want them to imagine it too." Ultimately, it was an expression of the new level of confidence, authenticity and connection that they were enjoying with God and his people.

The Imagination

In chapter 1 we outlined the longstanding and widespread call for the recovery of the place of the imagination in preaching. To a significant degree, the genesis of this research was a response to such calls and its main hypothesis was that through the use of *lectio divina* and Ignatian Gospel Contemplation the imagination would be enhanced in preaching. The discussion advanced a definition which posited that the imagination is more to do with recognizing the existing presence of God than with inventing something *ex nihilo*. Throughout the period when the participants preached and convened as a group, they experienced glimpses of the power of the imagination as described and defined in chapter 1. However, as principal researcher I noted that the participants' confirmation of the hypothesis tended to be more explicit when the discussion was not specifically centred on the imagination per se. Their reflection and experience of the prayers in relation to sermon preparation demonstrated moments when the imagination revealed God's presence in the way, for instance, that MacDonald[3] advocated. However, when I particularly focused the discussion on the imagination and enquired about their experience of it, their responses tended to become more circumspect and considered. It almost seemed that, in the first instance, the foray into the imagination was more experiential and instinctive than cognitive. The previous sections and chapters discussing the recovery of the group's first love for God and preaching, authenticity, dwelling with the text, and connecting in new ways with the congregation are evidence of the experiential and instinctive outworking of the imagination. These features demonstrated a greater awareness of their pastoral contexts and preaching ministries being energized by a new vision attentive to the presence and work of God. This new vision and level of awareness was predicated on an imagination fired and formed by deep engagement with the Scriptures. Later in this chapter, the discussion on *contemplatives in action* will also illustrate the expression of this. Even so, there were several occasions in the group meetings when I intentionally focused the discussion on the imagination, and we now turn our attention to a summary of those discussions.

At the second group meeting, six of the seven participants reported an initial revival in their imagination. Helen spoke of a far-reaching effect on her congregation. Within the parish, initiatives had already been underway when as part of this research she preached from Isaiah 58:1–12 (true fasting). With reference to the imagination she reflected, "So yes, there is that sense of spark . . . It's felt like it's captured our [congregational] global imagination. But I would say my gut reaction, my initial reaction, is to say that it feels like there's a bit more life and vision in there." Josie spoke about a change in her thinking during the time of sermon preparation: "But just having my vision altered somewhat as the starting place is turning out to be very helpful for me." At the halfway point of the research phase, the definition for the

---

3. MacDonald, *A Dish of Orts.*

imagination given in chapter 1 was a specific topic of discussion when the group met. Specifically, the participants were asked whether the definition "Imagination is the means of becoming attuned to the ongoing reality of the incarnation" resonated with them. One participant was unsure, while the remainder affirmed it to varying degrees. Rather than being more aware of the incarnation in her setting, Kathy described her experience as "working in the opposite way. Me being incarnated in the [biblical] story." This in itself was a wonderful finding, giving expression to Peterson's contention that the world of the Bible ought to be the defining one rather than life without reference to the Scriptures.[4] At the penultimate meeting, the group members were invited to complete a statement to gauge the effect of the imagination. Responses to the sentence "In my preaching, during this process, the imagination . . . " included:

- "Has been helped and encouraged."
- "Is a medium help."
- "Transports me into the biblical scene."
- "Expanded my understanding of what God is saying. There has been some growth and development in the realm of the imagination."
- "Has been a discovery in my preaching preparation. A place of blessing and inspiration."

In the last group meeting the definition for the imagination was revisited and the group members were asked whether their sense of the incarnation was heightened. Josie's comment was representative insofar as it was cautiously affirming, slightly contradictory and stopped short of outright endorsement:

> I didn't feel that [the prayer disciplines] enhanced my sense [of the incarnation]. I thought I'd just comment that I found it really powerful in one of the processes when you had the conversation with Jesus. And that was not something I was ever in the habit of doing in sermon preparation; that I did find very helpful and meaningful. But as an overall question about whether my sense of the incarnation was enhanced – not really.

As mentioned earlier, the more explicit and rich comments tended to emerge when participants were not asked directly about their experience in the area of the imagination. In general discussion, their reflection included natural references to it.

---

4. Peterson, *Eat This Book*.

At the last meeting, the focus was a review of the preceding four months of the exercise. Various questions and prompts were sent to the participants before the meeting so that they could prepare. From these questions and prompts some of the most telling comments about the imagination appeared, illustrating how the more explicit observations emerged without specifically focused questions on the imagination. One of these prompts was: "In the light of this experience, it seems good to the Holy Spirit and us . . ." This statement was intended to solicit observations which might be beneficial to the wider church. Michael's response was:

> I need to be at the other end of [the prayer] a little less me and more us [the congregation], in specifically asking the Holy Spirit for the Word that is going to translate in the incarnational experience and relationship that I've just had as a result of practising this and having it translated into a Sunday sermon for us, the congregation . . . I think these processes have been good in fanning the flame of imagination.

Michael's experience amounted to encountering the incarnation in fresh ways and being compelled to draw his congregation into that space. The positive effect of the imagination in this regard encompasses many of the earlier findings, such as growth in authenticity and connection with the congregation. Bob emailed his response as he was unable to be at the meeting and, interestingly, it was very similar to Michael's:

> The preacher must do all things possible to prepare and make available their heart and mind to allow God to speak into the community of faith . . . Preaching then becomes a vital process of life change both in the speaker and in the hearer. In the midst of this, the good use of imagination is a powerful means by which the message can touch and change lives for God's glory.

In the aftermath of the exercise it was clear that the power of the imagination, as it relates to an increased awareness of the presence and legacy of the incarnation, had begun to germinate. One further aspect of the imagination warrants comment: the place of wonder.

In the introduction and chapter 1, the laments of G. K. Chesterton and D. H. Lawrence concerning the lack of wonder in humanity were cited. Insofar as the historical-critical method is advanced as the only vanguard of sermon preparation, such a lack finds particular expression in the preaching ministry. This results in a lack of astonishment as the preacher studies and presents the

Scriptures and as the people of God hear it. The exercise is devoid of deep personal engagement and conviction.[5] This aspect of the imagination, wonder, was considered by the group members in the light of their prayer experience and preaching. A discernible increase in a sense of wonder was reported by five of the group members, with one participant spontaneously worshipping during their prayer and another being overwhelmed by the "wonder of grace." One participant tracked the experience of wonder from his time of prayer to the message and then to communion after it was preached. Furthermore, and more importantly, most of the group members attested to identifying the sense of wonder being experienced by their congregations. Frank redefined his and his congregation's experience as "surprise." He remarked, "The word I like [is] 'surprise', actually. That sense of surprise. More so than 'wonder' is how I would relate to what you are talking about. Surprise in many respects." Overall, this new experience of wonder could be discerned in much of the group's interaction during the course of the research. They did not always label it as such, but it took the form of new discoveries, renewed energy, deepening of pastoral relationships, a second naiveté towards the Scriptures and a sense of innovation in preaching them. As with most of the findings – and this was most certainly a common sentiment expressed at the last group meeting – there was the sense that they had experienced just a taste of a greater experience which is within reach. None of the findings were fully developed by the end of the research period but the glimpses were strong enough to convince them that the effects were not ephemeral. This proved also to be true of the last finding which will be discussed: *contemplatives in action*.

Contemplatives in Action

In chapter 2 the concept of *contemplatives in action* was discussed. To be a *contemplative in action* means that the fruit of prayer and contemplation finds expression in the world. The person is motivated by the revelation from their time of prayer and then seeks to be united to the mission of God in the world by discerning him in all things and obeying him. While *contemplatives in action* is a particular Jesuit construct undergirding Ignatian prayer, Benedictine development of *lectio divina* essentially advocated the same model with *ora, labora, lege* (pray, work, read). In his treatment of *lectio divina*, Mulholland[6]

---

5. Merton, *Opening the Bible.*
6. M. Robert Mulholland Jr., "Prayer as Availability to God," *Weavings* (1997): 20–26.

adds a movement after *contemplatio* which captures the sense of *contemplatives in action*: *incarnatio*. In one sense, *contemplatives in action* might appear to be an obvious point in that prayer ought to lead to action, but with time pressure and pastoral demands impacting on prayer (see chapter 4), the result can be a compartmentalizing of the elements of pastoral ministry. Hence, prayer in itself can be reduced to another task and its relationship with and effect on other aspects of ministry is not recognized. In the aftermath of engaging with *lectio divina* and Ignatian Gospel Contemplation, however, most participants discovered a distinct and ongoing effect in their wider pastoral ministries. While the effect was limited and varied from one group member to another, it was promising and emerged as a distinct finding. The first evidence of activity beyond the time of prayer was seen as participants attended to other aspects of their sermon preparation. In unguarded moments they experienced ongoing insights and engagement even though they were not in a designated time of prayer. This bore out Brou's observation,[7] cited in chapter 2, that preaching is an expression of the active life which emerges from contemplation. To the extent that they were *contemplatives in action*, participants embodied this in the initial context of the sermon.

As mentioned above, the first evidence of this was participants reporting that insights and thoughts which had not come during contemplation began to emerge during later stages of sermon preparation. Initially, while such experiences were prominent, their attribution to the ongoing effect of the contemplation was tentative. As the research phase continued, the connection between the time of prayer and these later revelations became clearer and stronger. Frank was one of the first participants to discover this dynamic, observing that there were poignant points of contact with his congregation when he preached the sermon. These points of contact, which had been long hoped for by Frank, had surfaced not necessarily during his prayer but during exegesis. He said, "There were things that came to me that hadn't come to me in the contemplation. But I still think there is something. I don't know what the connection is. Or even if there is a connection. I'm not sure. It's a coincidence: we can say that the time we spend [praying] results [in later material emerging]." Gwen was another who experienced this dynamic, and one incident especially bears reciting given the subsequent depth of insight. She was preparing a sermon on the imprisonment of Paul and Silas (Acts 16:16–34):

---

7. Brou, *Ignatian Methods of Prayer.*

I felt sent back to the Bible when I was in the middle of putting my sermon on the computer . . . It was like a door did open because I saw Paul and Silas in prison, and as we know, they couldn't sleep, so they began to sing songs and have a bit of a mission in the prison and these other people are listening too. And they are preaching to everybody. *Then* there is this great list of contrasts. There is an earthquake and the door comes open. But they can see a door in people's hearts. They don't bother with the door to leave the prison. And they can see when the gaoler gets a light to see if they are there – they probably start talking about Christ the light. And I could see all these contrasts. All these opportunities they could see. Their vision wasn't on the earthquake or getting out of prison. They could see the mission field there in the prison. They didn't bother running away. And the other thing the Lord showed me, well, I thought it was the Spirit showing me, was the gaoler washed their wounds. But they baptized him. So the water also . . . so a whole list of little contrasts there. But I didn't get that at the beginning but when the sermon was half done. So I thought the process sort of invades or seeps into other things. It's not just in a set box at this time or on this day.

At the last group meeting, when participants engaged with the statement "In the light of this experience, it seems good to the Holy Spirit and to us . . .," Gwen reflected further on this dynamic: "I suppose it is part of the contemplation cycle that is going on all the time. There is the opportunity to use the system further on." All five participants present at the last meeting attested to its presence and effect as unmistakable, with experiences being felt beyond the sermon and act of preaching itself.

While the theory of being *contemplatives in action* was frequently highlighted to the group, its materialization in their ministries seemed to happen of its own accord as opposed to any of the group members intentionally setting out to make it happen. Initially, the group was groping for vocabulary to describe an overarching and enduring effect from the prayer which influenced their sermons and permeated other aspects of ministry. Along with insights emerging in later sermon preparation, one of the initial indicators was as Gwen described it: "I think that the process has brought pockets of imagination in across my ministry rather than in the sermon itself." Helen at the same time observed integration between her prayer, sermon and wider congregational issues in the area of justice. Michael experienced what he referred to as the "great after-thought." He found that it did not stay in the realm of thinking but straddled his ministry and preaching. The ongoing effect gave direction to future sermons: ". . . whether it [the great after-thought] is an extra-something or was it *the* thing? But could the extra-something become *the* thing for next Sunday?" He went on to ponder approaching the one passage of Scripture from different angles in different sermons driven by the after-thought he had experienced. In many regards the participants' experience of being *contemplatives in action* was gestational. At the last group meeting Josie commented that she had experienced it to a limited extent but its full expression was stymied by her inability to invest more time in the prayer that would lead to such a lifestyle. Her experience is a fair representation of that of the group in general. The sense they had was, had they dedicated more time to prayer for sermon preparation and more time for this research to run, they would have experienced what it means to be *contemplatives in action* in even more striking ways.

In the discussion of the historical foundations of *contemplatives in action* in chapter 2, we considered Aquinas' and Nadal's analogy of Martha and Mary (Luke 10:38–42) as illustrative of the balance between action and contemplation. In the group members' experience their disposition as Mary (contemplation) positively shaped their disposition as Martha (activity) and in that order. Yet on balance, and as outlined in chapter 4, when wider pastoral issues and demands were imposed and the order was reversed, the anxious and frenetic disposition of Martha crowded out the quiet and prayerful disposition of Mary. To continue the analogy, when the order was Mary then Martha, the activity of Martha was of a different quality. Such activity was empowered and increased the participants' ability to make connections between the different elements of their overall ministry, which had a cumulative effect of being visionary. As already quoted, Helen described such moments as capturing her congregation's "global imagination." Such moments encapsulated von Balthasar's example of Jesus' rhythm and integration of contemplating the Father and then embodying his Word (see chapter 2).[8]

To some extent, being *contemplatives in action* serves as a catch-all concept for most of the positive findings in this research. The renewed sense of authenticity as preachers, described in chapter 3, is an expression of being a *contemplative in action*. The preacher is more present and engaged before the people of God. This relates also to the experience of a new sense of connecting

---

8. Von Balthasar, *Essays in Theology II.*

with the congregation, as described at the beginning of this chapter. Also, insofar as there was an increase in the outworking of the imagination in the context of pastoral ministry, with an accompanying heightened awareness of God and a sense of wonder, this too demonstrated something of what it means to be a *contemplative in action*. Even the difficulty of translating insights from prayer to the sermon, as described in chapter 4, is spoken to by this ideal. The intent of praying the Scriptures is to incarnate them as a follower of Christ by being empowered by the Spirit of Christ. The notion of being a *contemplative in action* was glimpsed by the group during the process and presented an aspiration at the end of the research phase. To use the exodus as an analogy, they were able to spy out the Promised Land (Num 13). They identified some giants but were able to return with a good report that it is indeed a land flowing with milk and honey. However, by the end of the research, they were yet to truly take up permanent residence in this space.

In this chapter, we have considered how group members enjoyed a new sense of connection with their congregations garnished by a biblically nourished imagination and expressed, to a limited extent, as *contemplatives in action*. Insofar as the definition of the imagination touched on an increased awareness of the presence of God, we began to see the start of something but needed more time. As the research progressed, the participants grasped my proposed definition of the imagination, but I suspect that in unguarded moments their notion that the imagination is more about make-believe and fantasy subtly hampered this. When people speak of the imagination there can be a tendency for them to instinctively remove themselves from being a part of what is imagined. They adopt the stance of an observer and are not intimately involved in the vision. My working definition of the imagination was formulated with the works of MacDonald[9] and Newman[10] as strong reference points. That definition read, "Imagination is the means of becoming attuned to the ongoing reality of the incarnation." I believe that this definition is too clumsy and that a tighter definition would have helped simplify matters. In the light of the research, my revised definition is, "A biblically nourished imagination discerns the legacy of the incarnation and presence of

---

9. MacDonald, *A Dish of Orts*.

10. John Henry Newman, *Grammar of Assent* (New York: Doubleday, 1955); Michael Paul Gallagher, "Newman on Imagination and Faith," first published 2002, accessed 30 October 2009 at http://www.plaything.co.uk/gallagher/academic/newman_imagination.html; Gallagher, "Theology and Imagination."

the kingdom." Even so, it would have been valuable to suspend offering the group a definition of the imagination at all. Instead, I believe it would have proved more fruitful to offer the group the contributions of writers such as MacDonald and Newman, and at the conclusion of the research invite the group to write their own definition of the imagination. Evidence that this would have been a good strategy was that when group discussion did not intentionally focus on the effect of the imagination, participants naturally volunteered positive insights about it. The imagination as nurtured by the two prayer disciplines was beginning to emerge.

6

Back to the Future: Twenty-First-Century Answers for First-Century Questions

During the six times that the group met, I did not always reveal my thoughts but instead, as principal researcher, endeavoured to facilitate discussion by creating as much open space as possible. Hence, the previous three chapters have largely reported group members' experiences and reflection rather than my own. In this concluding chapter, I will include myself in the material and use "we" as I agree with the findings.

This research engaged twelfth- and sixteenth-century models of prayer for a twenty-first-century context. To put it another way, pre-modern and early-modern forms of engaging with Scripture were applied to a post-modern context. Wright highlights the importance of formulating what it means to be a Christian today in the light of church history yet without living in that past and mistakenly wrestling with the issues of those times. He states:

> We must draw on wisdom from the past without imagining that our questions are identical with those faced by Luther or Calvin . . . or for that matter by Aquinas or Ignatius Loyola. Or for that matter, by John Henry Newman . . . We are in uncharted waters. And they are a lot deeper than some contemporary debaters seem to realize.[1]

---

1. N. T. Wright, *Scripture and the Authority of God* (London: SPCK, 2005), 14–15.

In a similar vein, Northcutt[2] laments the lack of attention given to the classics of Christian spirituality by contemporary preachers. She makes the incisive point that paying attention to, say, sixteenth-century wisdom does not mean retreating to a sixteenth-century worldview any more than exegeting Scripture results in retreating to a first-century worldview. So has this research exercise, by drawing on twelfth- and sixteenth-century spirituality, resulted in a Spirit-inspired twenty-first-century worldview? Or are the findings, at best, nothing more than a passing novelty, or, at worst, more fitting for a bygone era? Wright[3] provides a challenge that is helpful as we appraise this: "[T]he trick to aim for is to recover the first-century questions and try to give twenty-first-century answers, rather than taking sixteenth-century questions and giving nineteenth-century answers."[4] What are the first-century questions to which this research offers twenty-first-century answers?

The account of the disciples on the road to Emmaus (Luke 24:13–35) provides not only first-century questions but questions asked on day one of the post-resurrection era. On that first Easter day, the two disciples began their journey to Emmaus bewildered and saddened by the events of the previous three days. As the resurrected Christ walked with them unrecognized, he questioned them and their understanding of all that had happened. The ebb and flow of the conversation in this gospel account offers a means by which to consider the twenty-first-century answers provided by the reliance on two ancient forms of prayer. Three main questions emerge from this post-resurrection account and the corresponding answers are contained in each of the three chapters outlining the findings of this research (chaps 3, 4 and 5):

- **First Emmaus Question:** "What are you discussing with each other while you walk along?" (Luke 24:17)
- **Response:** Chapter 3 – "Renewal"

- **Second Emmaus Question:** "Was it not necessary that the Messiah should suffer these things and then enter into his glory?" (Luke 24:26)
- **Response:** Chapter 4 – "Repositioning"

---

2. Kay L. Northcutt, *Kindling Desire for God: Preaching as Spiritual Direction* (Minneapolis: Fortress, 2009).

3. N. T. Wright, "Q and A with Bishop Wright on 'Justification'," Ben Witherington on the Bible and Culture, Beliefnet. 2009, accessed 9 September 2010 at http://blog.beliefnet.com/bibleandculture/2009/06/q-and-a-with-bishop-wright-on-justification.html.

4. While the context of this particular comment by Wright is a discussion relating to justification, it articulates an incisive challenge to this research.

- **Third Emmaus Question:** "Were not our hearts burning within us while he was talking to us on the road, while he was opening the scriptures to us?" (Luke 24:32)
- **Response:** Chapter 5 – "Reorientation"

First Emmaus Question: "What are you discussing with each other while you walk along?"

Once Jesus drew near to the two on the road to Emmaus (Luke 24:15) he enquired about the nature of their discussion. Their sadness was matched only by their bewilderment at this mystery traveller's question. "Then one of them, whose name was Cleopas, answered him, 'Are you the only stranger in Jerusalem who does not know the things that have taken place there in these days?'" (24:18). Jesus probes further, asking, "What things?" (v. 19). The answer given to Jesus' line of questioning is essentially a reasonable summary of the gospel, with its inclusion of an acknowledgement of the resurrection, albeit at that early time and in those disciples' comprehension still in the realm of an astounding rumour (vv. 19–24). The two disciples were able to articulate the features of Christ's ministry, but only somewhat incompletely, as they were yet to comprehend the legacy of the incarnation: resurrection.

At the commencement of this research and as a group, we were not too dissimilar from the two disciples in this story. This initial question of Jesus' – "What are you discussing with each other while you walk along?" – invites us to give an account of our current position before the gospel. It found us able to articulate the features of the gospel and our response to it as preachers, but there was a sense of incompleteness in our outworking of that. We affirmed our sense of call and commitment to communicating the gospel, but found it hampered by a perceived loss in our devotion to God and in our proper attention to the call to preach. Like the two in Luke 24, we too could articulate the essence and nuances of the gospel, but we found ourselves in a place where the experience of that gospel had been eroded by other forces and we were muted. Our discussion in response to Jesus' question was marked by sadness as we considered the forces of consumerism and biblical illiteracy within our congregations. We discussed the desire to hone our preaching gifts and skills and to truly connect with our congregations. However, in the midst of the pressures of pastoral ministry, we keenly felt the temptation of pragmatism, which entices us to make shortcuts in our sermon preparation and delivery.

In the early stages of the research, we could subsequently answer Jesus' first-century question by stating that our discussion with each other as we "walked along" included observations of new life within our preaching ministries. We noted a growing and renewed sense of authenticity which emerged from dwelling in Scripture through the agency of the two prayer disciplines. Just as the two disciples in Luke 24 had their grief tempered by the then astounding rumour of the resurrection, so we too had our initial difficulties tempered by early and exciting encounters with the One who had drawn near on the road we were walking. Through *lectio divina* and Ignatian Gospel Contemplation, we had begun to keep the Word of Christ, and we found that he was taking up residence in our lives in new ways. Jesus' words proved true: "Those who love me will keep my word, and my Father will love them, and we will come to them and make our home with them" (John 14:23).

Second Emmaus Question: "Was it not necessary that the Messiah should suffer these things and then enter into his glory?"

When Jesus posed this question to the two travellers, it was by way of sharp challenge to their response to his first question. Their understanding of the events of Easter and their comprehension of the sweep of Scripture were found wanting. He subsequently expounded the Hebrew Scriptures to illuminate their understanding about his fulfilment of them (24:27). This second question operates as a rebuke and jolts the listener to the centrality of Christ and his mission. The effect of the question is corrective and as a rhetorical device demands examination of one's theological understanding and practice. This question encourages us to examine whether we faithfully represent and advance the contours, demands and promise of the gospel in our preaching. With regard to this research, the second question from Luke 24 follows on from the group's reasons for beginning the research and their initial findings (chapter 3). As a sharp challenge it demands our attention in evaluating whether we are accurately preaching the message of Christ in accordance with the Scriptures. If the first question seeks to determine the participants' initial position with reference to their spiritual state and preaching ministries, this second question seeks to test whether any necessary repositioning has taken place. This second question and movement in the story of the disciples on the road to Emmaus is the crucible of examination of our own understanding and practice over and against the message of the gospel, especially as it relates to the cross. A summary of chapter 4 forms the group's response to this question.

In chapter 4, four main themes were discussed. The first two were the struggle to find time to pray in the midst of pastoral demands and the struggle to decide which insights from the prayer were appropriate to preach about. These two struggles were offset in some measure by two other themes: the value of the Third Prelude from Ignatian Gospel Contemplation and the place of exegesis. Taken as a whole, these four considerations can be entitled the "pathology of the preacher." This pathology is the response to the second question posed from Luke 24 and it suggests that we have serious work to do. That pathology consists of a preacher who is conscientious and deeply concerned about congregational health but is undermined by wider pastoral demands which conflict with prayerful preparation of the sermon. To the extent that wider pastoral leadership duties sidetrack the preacher from the task of prayerful study there is a corresponding deep sense of guilt, tension and frustration. The pathology of the preacher as discovered by this research includes a person who hears God but has a struggle in deciding whether such revelations ought to be preached. In this research, this struggle was intensified by Kiwi cultural norms of restraint and modesty. Furthermore, the preacher demonstrated over-sensitivity to the dangers of eisegesis and this contributed to the suppression of otherwise valid insights which could have contributed to sound theological content for the sermon. However, the experience of grace by virtue of the Third Prelude and attention to sound exegesis helped the preacher navigate these difficulties. While this pathology is evident from the specific regime of this research, I suggest that to a large measure the group's experience is typical and that our pathology as preachers would be experienced by many in pastoral ministry today the world over.

Furthermore, with regard to the question in Luke 24 and its rhetorical nature, our struggle with committing time to prayer prevents us from answering completely positively. Just as the two disciples in Luke 24 must have done, we too would stare blankly at Christ as he rebukes our foolishness and slowness of heart to comprehend and attend to the message of Scripture (24:25). For as long as we continue to be unable to commit to uninterrupted and focused sermon preparation for a given sermon, we are unable to truly plumb the gospel message for that occasion and the people present. Our realization of the extent of the hourly pressures and distractions upon us as pastors endeavouring to prepare sermons came as a genuine shock to the group. Its continuance, our lack of strategy to combat it and hence our compliance in perpetuating such a pressured situation is a scandal. We have accepted that the demands upon our time, which are in severe conflict with prayerful sermon preparation, are the norm and that any attempt to change that would be unrealistic. To the extent that the demise of the volunteer culture affects our particular congregations, we have tended to attempt to fill the gap. It takes courage to resist the temptation to invest time and energy to fill such vacuums, especially when that time and energy are being plundered from sermon preparation. This research reoriented the group to the primacy of prayer and immersion in the Scriptures and the fact that the genesis of life and faith emerge from them. Hopefully, the insights and experiences of this research will galvanize us to be defiant in the face of all that seeks to usurp legitimate attention to our primary ministry task. As principal pastoral leaders in our congregations, surely the best way to model confidence in the gospel and trust in God is through a living engagement with his Word. As a group we certainly tasted the richness of that through *lectio divina* and Ignatian Gospel Contemplation, and it began to aid the rehabilitation of preaching as a priority.

As mentioned in the description of the pathology of the preacher, our response to the challenge of the second stated question from Luke 24 is partially muted due to our Kiwi cultural traits and lack of confidence in translating insights from prayer to the sermon. Yet the sovereignty and love of God in presenting particular graces in answer to the prayer of the Third Prelude proved to be a wonder. This inspired us to break through unhelpful uncertainties and reticence and occupy new places as preachers. We enjoyed the assurance offered to us through our exegetical training from yesteryear and the instincts honed since. Our experience positions us to confidently say that *lectio divina* and Ignatian Gospel Contemplation are at their best when in concert with sound exegetical conventions. However, we maintain that prayerful engagement with the Scriptures needs to precede exegetical work. This confirms Merton's call for two levels of understanding concerning Scripture, but reverses his order.[5] Particular insights gained from prayer need to be tested yet also not dismissed prematurely as eisegesis. Indeed, it would be valuable for more work to be invested in the definition and place of eisegesis as a complement to these two prayer disciplines and exegesis. Northcutt[6] uses the terms "precritical naïveté: contemplation" and "precritical

---

5. Merton, *Opening the Bible*.
6. Northcutt, *Kindling Desire for God*.

Scriptural naïveté" to capture the essence and balance of what is being advocated in this research. These terms draw attention to contemplation and dwelling with the text prior to critical exegetical study. "Precritical naïveté: contemplation" privileges "'felt experience' . . . emotions and felt concerns";[7] "precritical Scriptural naïveté" "seeks to mend the head/heart, cognitive/ affective split"[8] which can hamper preachers post-theological training and which was prominent in our experience upon commencing this research. In our experience, this constellation of the experience of grace, exegetical timing and technique, and a more relaxed view of eisegesis, position the preacher to answer affirmatively in response to the rhetorical question of Luke 24 in view: specifically, that the contours, demands and promise of the gospel are perceived and the presence of Christ experienced.

One final thought requires expression as it relates to Jesus' question "Was it not necessary that the Messiah should suffer these things . . . ?" The events of the cross have proved consistently troublesome for disciples, let alone for those who do not believe. From Peter's clash with Jesus at Caesarea Philippi (Mark 8:31–33) to Paul's description that the cross can be a stumbling block or foolishness (1 Cor 1:21–25), it nevertheless remains the power and wisdom of God, and all who follow Christ are distinguished by it (Mark 8:34). Rather than being discouraged by the pathology of the preacher as described earlier, we can find peace in the very existence of our failings and struggles insofar as we subject them to the theology of the cross. The difficulties we face as preachers serve as an occasion to redefine the ideal of a preacher in the light of the cross, just as the disciples' ideal of a Messiah required redefinition in the face of the cross's apparent failure. Maybe our perceived failings are the raw material by which our ambitions as preachers are challenged and renewed by the God of the cross who uses flawed humans as his spokespeople (1 Cor 1:26–31):

> Consider your own call, brothers and sisters: not many of you were wise by human standards, not many were powerful, not many were of noble birth. But God chose what is foolish in the world to shame the wise; God chose what is weak in the world to shame the strong; God chose what is low and despised in the world, things that are not, to reduce to nothing things that are, so that no one might boast in the presence of God. He is the

---

7. Ibid., 140.
8. Ibid., 141.

source of your life in Christ Jesus, who became for us wisdom from God, and righteousness and sanctification and redemption, in order that, as it is written, "Let the one who boasts, boast in the Lord."

The two prayer disciplines proved to be vehicles by which we keenly felt our human limitations in our pursuit of love for and service of God. Rather than fantasizing and pursuing a preacher's version of El Dorado, a place of unbridled riches of insights which are gained with ease, we instead "boast all the more gladly of [our] weaknesses, so that the power of Christ may dwell in [us]" (2 Cor 12:9). So the very presence of flaws is an occasion to celebrate the visitation of God as we are sanctified to another degree into the image of the Son. While we employed *lectio divina* and Ignatian Gospel Contemplation with the intention of mining the treasures of Scripture, what was unexpected was the way they exposed our humanity and emphasized our need of the cross. Thus *lectio divina* and Ignatian Gospel Contemplation facilitated the rhythm of grace of dying and rising, although we did not always perceive it.

Third Emmaus Question: "Were not our hearts burning within us while he was talking to us on the road, while he was opening the Scriptures to us?"

This third question from Luke 24, again essentially rhetorical, is the capstone of all that has transpired. The two disciples began the journey sad and bewildered, then had their understanding of the Christ-event reinterpreted, and by journey's end had their vision transformed. The question marvels at the change experienced and is echoed by the Catholic catechism, which draws on Ignatius' wisdom, describing the effect of contemplation: "[We learn] the 'interior knowledge of our Lord', the more to love him and follow him."[9] The effect of walking with Jesus is evident in the gospel account, but was such an effect evident in this research exercise? In Luke 24, this question is strategically placed as it looks back to the experience on the road with Christ and then serves as motivation for the two disciples to immediately return to Jerusalem. Once there, they bear witness to the resurrection with the Eleven and others present (24:33–35).

This final question challenges us as a group to give an account of the nature of our experience during the four months of our fieldwork and of what we are

---

9. US Catholic Church, *Catechism of the Catholic Church*, 715.

motivated to do now. If the second question from Luke 24 was a crucible of examination, this third question serves as an occasion to ponder the overall effect. Furthermore, the first question clarified our hopes and demeanour at the beginning of this research and revealed our initial discoveries; the second question highlighted the helps and hindrances in the process of attempting to align ourselves more with the Scriptures; the third question is the moment of honesty as to whether we can attest to a living encounter with Christ through it all. The findings described in chapter 5 are the response to this third and telling question.

By the time the two disciples neared Emmaus they had undergone a transformation. However, their companion appeared to be continuing on beyond the village and they pleaded with him to stay (24:28–29). By this time their hearts, which had been heavy with grief, were now inflamed by the exposition of Scripture and the presence of Christ. They wanted to hear and experience more. As a group, we too shared the sense that the journey was ending too soon and we desired more time to hear and experience Christ. Indeed, this proved to be one significant limitation of the research exercise; four months was not long enough. By the end of the fieldwork, group members frequently commented that they had experienced the beginning of something great. The phrase "if there had been more time" littered our last group meeting.

As principal researcher I had determined the period of four months in my initial research proposal, taking into consideration the timetable concerning submission of my thesis. With hindsight, I suspect that a period of twelve months would have proved even more effective in enabling the fruit of *lectio divina* and Ignatian Gospel Contemplation to become more engrained. The group members highly valued meeting with each other and discussing the advances and difficulties encountered. However, in my planning, any prediction of the richness of this process was overshadowed by my anxiety that requiring participants to adhere to a new regime of sermon preparation for four months, let alone longer, might be asking too much of them. Ironically, this concern was the very representation of the subsequent finding about wider pastoral responsibilities crowding out prayer and study of the Scriptures. Yet at the last group meeting, the tenor of our discussion was tantamount to pleading with Christ to stay with us longer and to saying to one another, "Were not our hearts burning within us while he was talking to us on the road, while he was opening the scriptures to us?" The desire for more could have translated to a longer period of fieldwork. To put it in perspective, we were considering theory which enjoys 500–1500 years of reflection, and we spent four months engaging with it.

The issue of the length of time for the fieldwork somewhat impacted the hypothesis and findings concerning the imagination. Again, Luke 24 serves as an appropriate analogy in that, just as our eyes were opened and we recognized Christ with us at the table, he vanished (24:31). Just as we began to sharpen our understanding of the imagination and recognize how it related to the prayer disciplines, the fieldwork phase ended. Yet despite these limitations, we experienced enough of the power of the imagination through the utilization of *lectio divina* and Ignatian Gospel Contemplation to be able to say, "Were not our hearts burning within us?" There was a discernable difference in our awareness of the legacy of the incarnation and our imaginations were inflamed to a marked and helpful degree. Our vision and experience were expanded and we became more energized and animated in preaching to our congregations. We felt compelled to communicate to them not only what we had learned during our sermon preparation but also something of *how* we had learned it. On occasions, as we preached, we described our prayer experience and in the moment of preaching facilitated a similar experience for them.

The effect of this included a new sense of connection with our congregations. Our sermons contained a different quality of content which was vibrant and inviting. It would be true to say that as a people of God we saw glimpses of Pentecost, and as the Word was preached, together we dreamed dreams and saw visions (Joel 2:28–32; Acts 2:17). Associated with this was a particular by-product of the imagination: a sense of wonder. Both participants and congregations experienced a thrill of wonder at the majesty and grace as a result of encountering God's message through the Scriptures. This melded preacher and congregation as the preached Word facilitated God's work among them. Further development and occurrence of this dynamic could be the means to inspire congregations to be aggressive in liberating preachers from other pastoral demands which compete for their attention to prayer and study.

Upon the disciples' recognizing Jesus, the final act on the road to Emmaus was the two disciples returning that very hour (24:33–35) to Jerusalem to bear witness to the resurrection. The question they asked each other identified the change effected during their journey and inspired them to retrace their steps, even though it was likely evening and unsafe to travel. To the extent that as a group our hearts also burned within us, we too undertook such a journey. The Jesuit concept of *contemplatives in action* parallels the return to Jerusalem of the disciples in Luke 24. We too found that our prayer experience translated into action that influenced the sermon and went beyond it. While the aforementioned limitation of time inhibited full realization and reflection of this dynamic, we identified its presence enough to confirm that something extraordinary had germinated. The previous comments relating to a new sense of connection with our congregations was in part due to the effects of finding ourselves as *contemplatives in action*. The change in our thinking and approach as a result of prayer permeated wider ministry responsibilities and influenced them. Again, the problem of wider pastoral demands eroding prayer and study time finds a response here. By being *contemplatives in action* and influencing ministry concerns apart from preaching, we can see that primary attention to *lectio divina* and Ignatian Gospel Contemplation does not necessarily result in the neglect of responsibilities but rather reconfigures and revitalizes them. However, such a practice involves more than changing our method of ministry: it means to embrace a lifestyle. It also requires more than the minister or pastor to determine this: it needs the commitment of the congregation.

Yet, if there is to be a divine conflagration among the people of God, a spark must first be felt by preachers. This third Emmaus road question wants to know if the engagement with the Scriptures is more than study and prayer at set times. The question is replete with biblical meaning, reference and heritage. The image of walking and talking with God continues the tradition from the garden of Eden (Gen 3:8) through the announcement of Immanuel ("God is with us," Matt 1:23) to the first intimate resurrection word spoken in the garden: "Woman, why are you weeping? Whom are you looking for?" (John 20:15). The reference to burning hearts encapsulates the enduring symbol of God's presence as represented by fire throughout Scripture. It casts the mind back to Moses before the burning bush (Exod 3:1–6), Isaiah's call sealed by a burning coal (Isa 6:1–8), and Jesus' dramatic declaration "I came to bring fire to the earth, and how I wish it were already kindled! " (Luke 12:49). The placement and spirit of the third question insist that any claim to have encountered Christ must involve the experiential. He is the God with us who comes with fire and speaks. Earlier we cited a paraphrase of Karl Rahner's[10] conviction: "Tomorrow's devout person will either be a mystic – someone who has 'experienced' something – or else they will no

---

10. Rahner, *Spirituality of the Church.*

longer be devout at all."[11] Throughout this research, whenever we engaged in *lectio divina* and Ignatian Gospel Contemplation we set foot on the road to Emmaus and by the grace of God we experienced him. In the main, like the original two on that road, while we had a destination in mind we utterly underestimated the journey along the way. We did not attempt to conjure up the presence of God, but he graced us with himself, even in the times when it seemed we were kept from recognizing him. He spoke to us and our people, and our hearts burned within us.

The story in Luke 24 finishes back in Jerusalem with the gathered community speaking of the resurrected Christ. The next pericope (Luke 24:36–48) begins with Jesus interrupting their conversation by appearing in their midst, saying, "Peace be with you." This biblical image of disciples gathered around the revelation and presence of the risen Christ, predicated on the exposition of Scripture and a living encounter with him, has been experienced throughout the ages. This research advances the belief that *lectio divina* and Ignatian Gospel Contemplation make a powerful contribution in aiding such an experience in the twenty-first-century church. The New Zealand Anglican Prayer Book provides a precise summary: "You have created us to hear your Word, to do your will and to be fulfilled in your love. It is right to thank you."[12]

---

11. Endean, *Karl Rahner and Ignatian Spirituality*, 63.
12. Church of the Province of New Zealand, *A New Zealand Prayer Book: He Karakia Mihinare o Aotearoa* (Auckland: Collins, 1989), 486.

Appendix A

Ignatian Gospel Contemplation on the Nativity

This is an example of the directions given to retreatants taking the Spiritual Exercises.[1] It is included here to illustrate how Ignatius encouraged freedom and liberty of the imagination so that the person could more readily be prayerfully located in the story. This is especially evident in the Second Prelude. However, such encouragement did not detract from the essential and recorded facts of the story as written in the Scriptures. The reference to "our Lady" is of course a Roman Catholic convention and should not be read as an imposition to those readers who are not Roman Catholic.

PRAYER. The usual preparatory prayer.

111. FIRST PRELUDE. This is the history of the mystery. Here it will be that our Lady, about nine months with child, and, as may be piously believed, seated on an ass, set out from Nazareth. She was accompanied by Joseph and a maid, who was leading an ox. They are going to Bethlehem to pay the tribute that Caesar imposed on those lands.

112. SECOND PRELUDE. This is mental representation of the place. It will consist here in seeing in imagination the way from Nazareth to Bethlehem. Consider its length, its breadth; whether level through valleys and over hills. Observe also the place or cave where Christ is born; whether big or little; whether high or low; and how it is arranged.

---

1. Excerpt from *The Spiritual Exercises of St. Ignatius of Loyola* by Louis J. Puhl, S. J. (Newman Press 1951). Reprinted with permission of Loyola Press. To order copies of this book call 1-800-621-1008 or go to www.loyolapress.com, 42–43.

113. THIRD PRELUDE. This will be the same as in the preceding contemplation and identical in form with it (i.e. This is to ask for what I desire. Here it will be to ask for an intimate knowledge of our Lord, who has become incarnate for me, that I may love him more and follow him more closely).

114. FIRST POINT. This will consist in seeing the persons, namely, our Lady, St Joseph, the maid, and the Child Jesus after His birth. I will make myself poor little unworthy slave, and as though present, look upon them, contemplate them, and serve them in their needs with all possible homage and reverence.

Then I will reflect on myself, that I may reap some fruit.

115. SECOND POINT. This is to consider, observe, and contemplate what the persons are saying, then to reflect on myself and to draw some fruit from it.

116. THIRD POINT. This is to see and consider what they are doing, for example, making the journey and laboring that our Lord might be born in extreme poverty, and that after many labors, after hunger, thirst, heat and cold, after insults and outrages, He might die on the cross and all this for me.

Then I will reflect and draw some spiritual fruit from what I have seen.

117. COLLOQUY. Close with a colloquy as in the preceding contemplation, and with the *Our Father*.

Appendix B

Participatory Action Research Method

Participatory Action Research

The method for this study is from the action research stable, specifically Participatory Action Research (PAR). PAR emerged in the 1970s with a focus on the marginalized and poor in the developing world, particularly regarding community renewal.[1] The purpose of PAR is to enhance the relationship between the individual and the community. The features of PAR which support this are its collaborative nature; its emancipatory potential; its self-critical process; its ability to investigate reality and change it; and its insistence on critiquing both theory and practice and transforming them.[2] Given that the participants of this research were preachers in live pastoral situations, PAR was favoured because it enabled their views and convictions about preaching to be respected and to influence the process. This method was especially exciting because participants had an opportunity to "undertake

---

1. Peter Reason, "Three Approaches to Participative Inquiry," in *Handbook of Qualitative Research*, ed. Norman K. Denzin and Yvonna S. Lincoln (Thousand Oaks, CA: Sage, 1994); Stephen Kemmis, and Robin McTaggert, "Participatory Action Research," in *Handbook of Qualitative Research*, ed. Norman K. Denzin and Yvonna S. Lincoln, 2nd ed. (Thousand Oaks, CA: Sage, 2000); Orlando Fals Borda, "Participatory (Action) Research in Social Theory: Origins and Challenges," in *Handbook of Action Research: Participatory Inquiry and Practice*, ed. Peter Reason and Hilary Bradbury (London: Sage, 2001), 27–37; Budd L. Hall, "I Wish This Were a Poem of Practices of Participatory Research," in *Handbook of Action Research*, 171–178; Peter Park, "Knowledge and Participatory Research," in *Handbook of Action Research*.

2. Kemmis and McTaggert, "Participatory Action Research"; Jean McNiff, Pamela Lomax and Jack Whitehead, *You and Your Action Research Project*, 2nd ed. (London: RoutledgeFalmer, 2003).

a formal, reflective process for their own development and empowerment,"[3] which was ideal for this project because it created a learning environment for participants yet enabled them to remain "open to surprises and responsive to opportunities."[4] Given the nature of working with Scripture and depending on the Spirit's guidance, PAR allowed for a sense of adventure. Furthermore, PAR was appropriate for this study because it has been described as a "way of life"[5] that goes beyond research methodology towards "a philosophy of life that would convert its practitioners into 'thinking-feeling persons.'"[6] Such a philosophy was in keeping with the hope of this study to enhance the engagement of preachers with the Scriptures and the people they serve.

However, PAR's origins in a context of those suffering marginalization raises a question in the pastoral context: "Surely it is the congregation who is at a disadvantage rather than the preacher?" While this could be the case, it is intriguing to note that in response to the question "What issue gave rise to you agreeing to be a part of this research?" participants articulated a sense of isolation and a degree of marginalization. They also expressed feelings of being silenced by the forces of consumerism in the congregation, congregational biblical illiteracy, and the constant struggle to find a healthy tension between nurturing personal devotional life and giving appropriate public expression to that through preaching. Furthermore, PAR is set apart from other action research methods in that the "non-experts" are involved.[7] The objection could be raised, "Surely preachers cannot be termed 'non-experts' in the light of their training?" While the participants involved were all professionally trained ordained ministers, their responses demonstrated a keen sense of dissatisfaction with the status quo and a desire for continued professional development. This sentiment was ably conveyed by one participant when he said, "I'm always enormously dissatisfied with my preaching and always had a sense that surely there is a better way of delivering this or doing this or being this." While every participant was competent in preaching, they all expressed enough dissonance concerning the challenges of preaching to warrant the use of PAR.

3. Michael Quinn Patton, *Qualitative Research and Evaluation Methods*, 3rd ed. (Thousand Oaks, CA: Sage, 2002), 183.

4. Louis Cohen, Lawrence Manion and Keith Morrison, *Research Methods in Education*, 5th ed. (London: RoutledgeFalmer, 2002), 229.

5. Quoted in Hall, "I Wish This Were a Poem," 174.

6. Borda, "Participatory (Action) Research," 31.

7. Park, "Knowledge and Participatory Research," 82.

While the method for this study contains sequential steps, it needs to be acknowledged that the nature of PAR means that the process can become messy and is self-propagating. To some extent, it is easier to discover PAR's philosophy rather than provide a detailed explanation of its steps.[8] "The criterion of success is not whether participants have followed the steps faithfully, but whether they have a strong and authentic sense of development and evolution in their practices, their understandings of their practices, and the situations in which they practice."[9] Indeed, even if a planned strategy appears to be an abysmal failure, the resultant reflection and personal learning are vindication.[10] PAR appeared to be well suited to this research given that its context is the fluidity, demands, opportunities and rigours of pastoral ministry. The following procedure was designed with the research topic in mind and in keeping faith with the broad contours of PAR, specifically an iterative cycle of planning, action and reflection. Also, the integrity of PAR was always kept in view by ensuring that the process remained truly participatory and collaborative.[11] While as facilitator I convened the group and provided resources and education about the process and the two approaches to praying the Scriptures, the group maintained control of the process and as participants were co-equal. They had a genuine voice in interpreting data, setting the direction of the research and drawing conclusions. A summary of what such participation and collaboration entailed was provided for each participant so they could ensure the process remained accountable.

The method developed for this study involved seven preachers joining me in the process of utilizing *lectio divina* and Ignatian contemplation as part of regular sermon preparation during the period from 7 February 2010 to 30 May 2010. While participants were ministers of separate churches, the shared commitment to and passion for preaching provided the initial commonality for the research. The group members met five times (23 February, 16 March, 20 April, 18 May and 29 June) to reflect on their experiences and to hone

---

8. Reason, "Three Approaches to Participative Inquiry."

9. Kemmis and McTaggert, "Participatory Action Research," 595; John Swinton and Harriet Mowat, *Practical Theology and Qualitative Research* (London: SCM, 2006).

10. McNiff, Lomax and Whitehead, *Your Action Research Project.*

11. John Heron and Peter Reason, "The Practice of Co-operative Inquiry: Research 'with' Rather Than 'on' People," in *Handbook of Action Research: Participative Inquiry and Practice,* ed. Peter Reason and Hilary Bradbury (London: Sage, 2001), 180–188; Michael Quinn Patton, *Qualitative Research and Evaluation Methods,* 3rd ed. (Thousand Oaks, CA: Sage, 2002).

future use of both approaches. This iterative cycle is diagrammatically represented in figure 1.

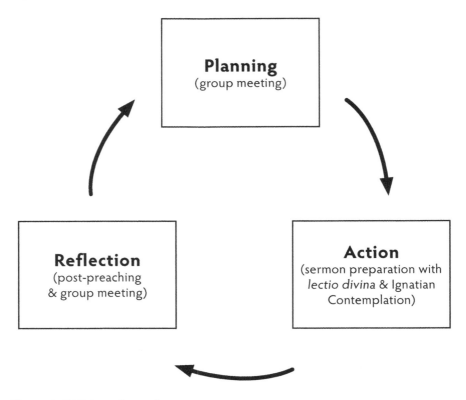

Figure 1: PAR iterative cycle

The group meetings were audiotaped and relevant sections transcribed, coded and analysed using NVivo-8 Qualitative Research software. The Australian College of Theology approved the thesis proposal and granted ethics clearance in March 2009.

One of the major criticisms of action research is the difficulty an observer can experience in attempting to validate and recover the research, given its dynamic and fluid nature.[12] Indeed, PAR has been described as "low-tech" research because it "sacrifices methodological sophistication in order to generate timely evidence that can be used and further developed in a real-

---

12. Kemmis and McTaggert, "Participatory Action Research"; Donna Champion and Frank A. Stowell, "Validating Action Research Field Studies: PEArL," *Systemic Practice and Action Research* 16, no. 1 (2003): 21–36.

time process of transformation."[13] Participants involved in action research are confronted with the immediacy and reality of their contexts and "*live with the consequences of the transformations they make.*"[14] Consequently, Kemmis and McTaggert assert that it is appropriate for practicalities which make critical sense to participants to take precedence over satisfying the criteria of those not living in the actual research context. Nevertheless, they acknowledge the need to strengthen action research by enhancing the range of evidence available for a third party to consider the research. In recognition of this concern, this particular study subscribes to the use of the mnemonic "PEArL," which stands for Participation, Engagement, Authority, Relationships and Learning:

> Crucially, the elements of the PEArL mnemonic offer the means for an individual who was not involved in the inquiry process to reflect upon and make a judgment about the authenticity of the inquiry process. It is this potential to involve "nonparticipants" that, in our opinion, makes PEArL such a powerful tool when making a judgment concerning the authenticity of a process of social inquiry.[15]

Hence, PEArL serves as a lens through which this PAR project can be viewed in order to enhance the authenticity and credibility of the research offered.

PEArL

The elements of PEArL and its application to this particular research project are as follows:

Participants

Explanation
This aspect speaks to the reasons for and criteria determining why participants were either included or excluded and the process by which they were recruited.

---

13. Kemmis and McTaggert, "Participatory Action Research," 591.

14. Ibid., 592, emphasis in original.

15. Champion and Stowell, "Validating Action Research Field Studies," 22. The "r" in PEArL is lower case as a way of emphasizing the prime importance of "relationships" within the enquiry process.

Application

For this research participants needed to be at least eighteen years of age and engaged in a regular preaching ministry to one congregation. Specifically, this translated to preaching to the same congregation at least three weeks out of every five. This specification was set to ensure that the research drew on a consistent and committed pastoral relationship which would supersede the sense of novelty when engaging in a new approach. Hence, the highs and lows of this exercise could be experienced and measured against the present congregation and any historical relationship with them. The age stipulation was set to signal that some life experience and training had been experienced. While a minimum of eighteen years was stated, it was realistic to expect that no one younger than twenty years would offer to participate. This is because it is unlikely that someone younger than twenty years of age would be in a regular preaching ministry preaching three weeks out of every five to the same congregation. Nevertheless, the possibility remained and so eighteen years was stipulated. There was no stipulation stated concerning gender, denomination, theological persuasion or ethnicity. This was to encourage as wide a selection of participants as possible. Due to the requirement to meet as a group during the fieldwork phase, participants needed to be ministering in the greater Auckland (NZ) area. This meant that no one would be more than thirty–forty-five minutes' drive from meeting venues.

Participants were recruited from three settings and groups. The first was a preaching group which had been meeting since 2003 in Auckland. This group consisted of ministers and lecturers in theological colleges who were committed to preaching. They met once a quarter and its membership ranged from ten to twelve attendees of various denominations. This group met for the purpose of discussing the trends, theology and practice of preaching. The second setting was the South Auckland Presbytery of the Presbyterian Church of Aotearoa New Zealand (PCANZ), of which I was a member. The third recruitment setting was a preaching seminar, "Kiwi-made Preaching," convened by the Langham Partnership in Auckland (April 2009). This seminar drew 220 attendees and permission was granted to recruit at this event. I conducted a workshop based on material gleaned from the early stages of this research and offered the opportunity for participation at the conclusion of the session. Together, the three different settings and groups produced a wide range of participants. All participants signed a consent form. A summary of information about the participants is shown in table 1.

Engagement

Explanation

This aspect of PEArL centres on the ways in which participants were empowered to engage with the process so as to have as full an involvement as possible:

> By making evident the methods and tools employed to engage people in the learning process, interested individuals can reflect upon the environment in which the learning took place. The methods of engagement also reflect other constraints on the inquiry process, such as the time permitted, the resources made available, or when meetings were held.[16]

This component also demonstrates the level of collaboration and participation enjoyed by members of the PAR group.

Application

An orientation and training day was held on 17 November 2009. Group members were schooled in *lectio divina* and Ignatian Gospel Contemplation over six hours. They were issued with a comprehensive booklet written specifically for the occasion and research (see appendix C). The booklet included summaries of each contemplative approach, further detailed explanations, key quotes and references, worksheets to record sermons preached (Feb–May 2010) and a bibliography. During the day participants engaged in two exercises of praying *lectio divina* and Ignatian Gospel Contemplation. Prior to the day, the question "What issue has given rise to you agreeing to be a part of this research?" was emailed to each participant. Participants came to the day with a prepared answer. This was for the purpose of discerning if the group enjoyed a shared task for the direction of the group. While the group shared a strong commitment to preaching, it was crucial for the integrity of PAR to determine other unifying reasons in order to facilitate high levels of ownership. Such reasons were established and a discussion of these can be found in chapter 3.

The participation criterion of preaching at least three weeks out of every five translated into at least ten sermons during February–May 2010. With this in mind, the group discussed the parameters of the exercise and established the following features:

---

16. Champion and Stowell, "Validating Action Research Field Studies," 29.

Name — All pseudonyms except for me: "Geoff."	Gender	Age Group	Denomination	Years in ministry	Years in current church	Recruited from	Exp of *lectio divina*	Exp of Ignatian Gospel Contemplation
Bob	Male	50–59	Presbyterian	27	7	Presbytery	Limited	Limited
Frank	Male	50–59	Baptist	12	4	Preaching group	Limited	Limited
Geoff	Male	40–49	Presbyterian	12	12	Presbytery	Good	Significant
Gwen	Female	60–69	Methodist	15	4¾	Langham	Limited	None
Helen	Female	40–49	Anglican	10	10	Preaching group	Limited	None
Josie	Female	30–39	Baptist	4½	4½	Preaching group	Limited	Limited
Kathy	Female	40–49	Presbyterian	7 mths	7 mths	Presbytery	Limited	None
Michael	Male	40–49	Presbyterian	7	5 mths	Presbytery	None	Good

Table 1: Personal profile and ministry experience of research participants

- That of the ten sermons required, *lectio divina* or Ignatian Gospel Contemplation would be utilized at least three times each in sermon preparation. The balance of the remaining four sermons would be at the discretion of each preacher.
- For each sermon, it was left to the discretion of each preacher to choose which Scripture passage to preach from.
- The group would meet once a month, with the last meeting held in June 2010.
- The group would decide the time, day of the week and venue for the meetings.

The participants agreed to adopt a semi-structured meeting regime to guide group meetings. They endorsed the following questions to engage with at each meeting:

- What has happened since we last met?
- What has worked and what needs reworking?
- What effect has there been on your role as a preacher?
- Is there anything you perceive which we are overlooking?

Authority

Explanation

The third element of PEArL is authority. This element seeks to clarify what authority group members possess as a part of the process, and the extent of this authority. Specifically, who authorized it? What elements were authorized and for what purpose? In short, this was establishing "the degree of 'self-governance'" of participants.[17] The presence of authority is important in that it ensures that learning outcomes are not dictated to the group but that they emerge organically. "During a social inquiry the learning outcomes are created by those involved as they find a way through their dilemma. The Action Researcher's role will be to *navigate* and manage the learning process so as to create some learning outcomes that are acknowledged to be valid."[18] The desire to develop expertise and effectiveness as preachers formed the group's sense of self-governance for the process. They experienced deficiencies in their own preaching ministries, yet also demonstrated courageous openness as to where such an exercise might lead.

---

17. Champion and Stowell, "Validating Action Research Field Studies," 30.
18. Ibid., emphasis in original.

Application

The most obvious and immediate sense of authority derived by participants came by virtue of their ordination vows. They saw involvement in this process as a way of fulfilling those vows and that it was expected and recognized that as ordained ministers, the pulpit was their responsibility alone. Furthermore, of the seven participants, four consulted with their congregational leadership body and received endorsement to be a part of the study. Overall, participants reported that such authority and endorsement allowed them to be involved for the purposes of self-care, collegiality and the enhancement of their preaching ministries. This translated to allowing them the scope to commit to meetings at whatever frequency was deemed necessary.

Relationships

Explanation

This component of PEArL is considered primary given the presence of "undeclared assumptions and beliefs operating, causing conflict and misunderstanding and, also, synergy and acceptance."[19] Invariably such relationships involve the aspect and expression of power. Champion and Stowell posit that it is helpful to utilize the metaphor that power is a commodity. "Applying this metaphor enables individuals to ask how power has been expressed within the situation and how these 'commodities' may be used and maintained. The metaphor also facilitates the recognition of any potential beneficiaries or victims of the intervention."[20] Given that PAR endeavours to transform a context, reflection on changes within existing relationships within that context provides important indicators of the nature of any transformation.

Application

Engagement with an exercise such as this has the potential to change existing relationships within the group as well as the relationships of preacher–congregation, preacher–Scripture and, most importantly, preacher–God. The change in these relationships could not be predicted, although obviously it was hoped that they would be enriched. Nevertheless, such change can involve the creation, death and resurrection of various relationships and so

---

19. Champion and Stowell, "Validating Action Research Field Studies," 31.
20. Ibid.

the potential for good and bad needed to be acknowledged. Also, attention to power as a commodity was given by regularly inviting the group to reflect on any perceived changes in their relationships as they related to power. The concepts of "power over," "power with" and "power within" were used as reference points and language to aid reflection.[21]

Learning

Explanation

Champion and Stowell emphasize the importance of making the learning outcomes available to those who are unable to be a part of the ongoing discussions and debates:

> Participants in the learning will have gained awareness of the perspective of others and the active process of engaging in discussion may engender an appreciation of the possibilities and constraints within a situation. However, debate alone cannot be considered a sufficiently inclusive method of achieving an appreciation of the situation. By recording the learning outcomes and also other elements within PEArL in some manner, individuals not involved, or who did not participate in the actual discussion, may be quietly supported in making their own judgments concerning the *authenticity* of the inquiry process.[22]

The "application" sections of this survey of the elements of PEArL are one attempt to fulfil the requirement of recording the features of PEArL present within this research.

Application

New discoveries and insights were expected to be unearthed by the iterative cycle of preaching sermons in the light of preparation informed by *lectio divina* and Ignatian Gospel Contemplation; by then meeting together to reflect on the experience, to collaborate and to plan; and then by returning to the pastoral context to preach. While several hypotheses and questions were present from the outset of this study, the very nature of PAR lent itself to the fact that particular learning could not be presumed. The learning is recorded in chapters 3, 4 and 5 so that those not privy to the discussions in the group

---

21. Martha Ellen Stortz, *PastorPower* (Nashville: Abingdon, 1993).

22. Ibid., 32, emphasis in original.

can still make a judgement about the validity, integrity and authenticity of this study. After each meeting, group members were sent summaries of the discussion and conclusions for their approval. When the occasion required observations of learning to be made from the perspective of the facilitator and author of this research, these were stated clearly.

In summary, PEArL not only provides a method for a third party to scrutinize the findings of PAR, it also provides helpful categories and vocabulary for the principal researcher and the participants in the PAR exercise to organize data. As the group met and experiences were reflected upon, the wide and varied material was marshalled with PEArL in mind. PEArL served the principles of PAR without imposing intractable categories upon it or doing violence to its dynamism. PEArL helped to guide group discussion, provided a framework to focus reflection and served as a template to analyse the data.

Appendix C

Preacher's Manual

Lectio Divina and Ignatian Contemplation in Preaching

Contents

Imagination

[The] major and too-little-remarked evil in our time is the systematic degradation of the imagination. The imagination is among the chief glories of the human ... Right now, one of the essential Christian ministries in and to our ruined world is the recovery and exercise of the imagination. **EUGENE PETERSON**

I have left out the most serious lack of all: imagination. Without imagination the preacher limps along on one leg. **WALTER BURGHARDT SJ**

We are the victims of a split between academic study and person-involving study. **JOHN GOLDINGAY**

The exegetes have taken away my Lord, and I know not where they have laid him. **WALTER BURGHARDT SJ**

We need to understand scripture historically. But we also need to be open to leaps of inspired imagination. **JOHN GOLDINGAY**

Imagination is the supreme work of [sermon] preparation. **G. CAMPBELL MORGAN**

[Imagination is] the God-power in the soul. **HENRY WARD BEECHER**

Fancy wrote "Mary had a little lamb" but inspired imagination wrote "The Lord is my Shepherd." Fancy creates a new world for you; imagination gives you insight into the old world. **WARREN WIERSBE**

The simplest and most basic way to meditate upon the text of Scripture is through the imagination. **RICHARD FOSTER**

What impact might a "recovery and exercise of the imagination" have upon our:

- engagement with Scripture,
- awareness of the Spirit,
- creation of the "sermon proposition,"
- authenticity as preachers,
- sense of wonder?

_____

_____

_____

_____

Distractions – expect them!

- Noise (internal & external)
- Memories
- Daydreaming
- Tiredness
- Haste
- Worry
- Boredom

There is no meditation without distraction. Return, then, to the reading. Concentrate on the key words.[1]

Go back to the Word, read on a bit further. Use the Word of God as your safeguard, your guide. Don't fight the devil; don't fight yourself. That is God's business.   **GABRIEL O'DONNELL**

Avoid the impact of distractions, simply write the verse without comment and/or write about what is happening. *Lectio divina* and Ignatian Contemplation were developed at least in part, to combat distractions!

---

1. Fr Bernado Olivera quoted in Pennington, *Lectio Divina*.

Lectio Divina

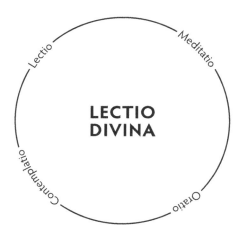

While *lectio divina* had already been practised by the church for 1,000 years, the format we use was developed by the monk Guido II (d. 1188).

Lectio – read the text

Meditatio – ruminate on the text

Oratio – pray in response to the text

Contemplatio – incarnate the text

Or we can think of it as nourishment

Lectio – solid food

Meditatio – chewing & breaking it up

Oratio – savouring it

Contemplatio – enjoying refreshment & sustenance

We come to lectio *not so much seeking ideas, concepts, insights, or even motivating graces; we come to* lectio *seeking God himself and nothing less than God.*   **W. BASIL PENNINGTON**

Luke 10:26
> "How do you read?" (e.g. AV, RSV, NASB, NIV) rather than
> "What do you read?" (e.g. NRSV)

Luke 10:26
> "How do you read?" invites participation and response;
> "What do you read?" amounts to a detached response.

Lectio divina is
- a way of reading that becomes a "way of living"
- a way of life that develops "according to the Scriptures"

Lectio divina is not 1-2-3-4 but . . .
- strands of the same cord
- different attitudes of the same gesture
- a dance
- a looping spiral
- dangerous chemical elements joining to form a helpful compound
- colours of the rainbow

If our convictions are so fragile that they cannot be exposed to alternative visions, then lectio divina *is not for us.*   **MICHAEL CASEY**

Selected Quotes Concerning *Lectio Divina*

With *lectio divina* firmly in view, Peterson proffers a solemn warning:

> The word of God is not my possession. The words printed on the pages of my Bible give witness to the living and active revelation of the God of creation and salvation, the God of love who became the Word made flesh in Jesus, and I had better not forget it. If in my Bible reading I lose touch with this livingness, if I fail to listen to this living Jesus, submit to this sovereignty, and respond to this love, I become arrogant in my knowing and impersonal in my behavior. An enormous amount of damage is done in the name of Christian living by bad Bible reading. *Caveat lector*, let the reader beware.[2]

Lectio *is a disciplined form of devotion and not a method of Bible study. It is done purely and simply to come and to know God, to be brought before His Word, to listen.*[3]

Lectio divina *is not a methodical technique for reading the Bible. It is a cultivated, developed habit of living the text in Jesus' name. This is the way, the only way, that the Holy Scriptures become formative in the Christian church and become salt and leaven in the world.*[4]

Lectio divina *is an element in a lifelong process of turning toward God: its effects are discernible only in the long term. Equally, the effects of the absence of lectio may not be apparent to us until it is too late.*[5]

Lectio divina *is an expression of my search for God: Sacred reading can be considered "successful" only if it causes me to drop my defences and allow God to touch my heart and change my life.*[6]

---

2. Peterson, *Eat This Book*, 85.
3. O'Donnell, "Reading for Holiness," 47.
4. Peterson, *Eat This Book*, 116.
5. Fiedler, "Lectio Divina," 69.
6. Casey, *Sacred Reading*, 62.

When you ask: "What is this book [Bible]?" you find that you are also implicitly being asked: "Who is this that reads it?"[7]

Lectio *has been described as a prayer that begins as a "dialogue" and ends as a "duet." Thus what begins as God addressing us and our responding leads eventually to an experience of union.*[8]

The Scriptures need to be read in the same spirit in which they were written, and only in that spirit are they to be understood. You will never reach an understanding of Paul until, by close attention to reading him and the application of continual reflection, you imbibe his spirit. You will never arrive at understanding David until by the actual experience you realize what the psalms are about . . . In every piece of Scripture, real attention is as different from mere reading as friendship is from entertainment, or the love of a friend from a casual greeting.[9]

7. Merton, *Opening the Bible*, 27.
8. O'Donnell, "Reading for Holiness," 48.
9. William of St Thierry quoted in Squire, *Asking the Fathers*, 124.

Lectio (reading aloud)

A passage of Scripture is chosen as the focus of *lectio divina*.

To read the Scripture through the agency of *lectio divina* requires, in the first instance, an appreciation of how it was carried out centuries ago. When *lectio divina* was employed in ancient times, people did not read as we do now: silently and mentally.[10] The text was read aloud and, therefore, heard. "One reads, in the ancient sense of that word, with one's mouth and one's ears,"[11] and in antiquity reading rested on the sense that the text was primarily proclaimed and heard rather than seen. Dwyer expresses bewilderment that the essence of *lectio divina* has been lost in translation across the centuries and today. He challenges the translation of *lectio divina* as "spiritual reading," given that so many in the early church were illiterate. "So it was never meant to be what we made it. What was it? *Lectio divina* was the art of listening."[12]

The selection of the Scripture passage ought not to be haphazard or piecemeal; "[such] textual 'roulette' can . . . tempt us to use *lectio* for some immediate gratification."[13] In order to honour the relational dynamic of *lectio divina*, it is advisable to stay with an entire book of the Bible.[14] Then the person begins by reading aloud in a slow and careful manner, as one might read poetry. As the reader listens, the text begins its work of triggering "memories and associations that reside below the threshold of awareness."[15] The intent is to listen for a particular word or phrase which captures the attention especially. This may happen in the first sentence read or only after repeated readings.[16] "How far along we get in the text is less important than how open we are to the power and message if the text is leading us to authentic communication with God."[17] *Lectio divina* depends on a leisurely, careful and attentive reading pace.

10. O'Donnell, "Reading for Holiness"; Fiedler, "Lectio Divina"; Pennington, *Lectio Divina*; Canham, *Praying the Bible*; Russell, "Why Lectio Divina is Difficult"; Peterson, *Eat This Book*.

11. O'Donnell, "Reading for Holiness," 46.

12. Dwyer, "Many Paths to Prayer."

13. O'Donnell, "Reading for Holiness," 48.

14. Ibid., no page number; Casey, *Sacred Reading*.

15. Casey, *Sacred Reading*, 83.

16. Pennington, *Lectio Divina*.

17. O'Donnell, "Reading for Holiness," 48.

Lectio – read the text aloud
- Commit your time in prayer
- Choose a passage of Scripture
- Read it *aloud* several times
- Listen for that *one* word or phrase that captures your attention

Meditatio (meditation)

Just as true *lectio* depends on giving attention to tracts of Scripture in context, "Meditation [*meditatio*] is the aspect of spiritual reading that trains us to read Scripture as a connected, coherent whole, not a collection of inspired bits and pieces."[18] The word or phrase which has arrested the attention during *lectio* is ruminated over. It is questioned, pondered, repeated, explored, examined; it is meditated upon. The imagination will come into play as images form, guided by the text at hand and enriching this moment of being formed by the Word.[19] "Meditation is the prayerful employ of imagination in order to become friends with the text."[20] However, *meditatio* is not a time of inventing fanciful and fictitious thoughts and visions.

Meditatio – ruminate on the text
    Question, explore, examine the word/phrase
- Why of all the words and phrases has this one caught my attention?
- Why does it appeal? Or challenge?
- How does it make me feel?
- What thoughts come to mind?

Meditatio is . . .
- when the reality of God's story comes to bear upon the person
- being attentive to what God has done in Christ and how by his Spirit he now calls forth a response
- a moment of Christ-centred honesty and submission

---

18. Peterson, *Eat This Book*, 100.
19. O'Donnell, "Reading for Holiness."
20. Peterson, *Eat This Book*, 101.

Oratio (prayer)

Oratio is the moment when the weight and reality of the story of God come to bear upon the person. *Meditatio* is being attentive to what God has done in Christ and how now by his Spirit he calls forth a response from the disciple. Rather than *meditatio* launching a person into flights of fancy, true *meditatio* earths a person in the context of the Word. It is a moment of Christ-centred honesty and submission.

"*Lectio* [*divina*] has been described as a prayer that begins as a 'dialogue' and ends as a 'duet'. Thus what begins as God addressing us and our responding leads eventually to an experience of union."[21] *Oratio* is the place where dialogue begins to become a duet; where a response to the Word begins to lead to union with God.

Oratio is also the place of integrity. *Lectio divina* as a whole is a process of aligning ourselves with the purposes of God. "The major determinant of prayer or *lectio* is our fidelity to seeking God in everyday behavior. It is no good being fervent in reading if we are slack in living."[22] *Oratio* is that place of intentional response to God in whatever way is most fitting. It can be the place of fierce temptation as in the garden of Eden (Gen 3); the dark wrestling of the garden of Gethsemane (Matt 26); and/or the joy of the garden of the tomb (John 20).

Oratio – we pray the text
    Pray in response
- Thanksgiving
- Request
- Repentance
- Praise
- Intercession
- Any kind of prayer

21. O'Donnell, "Reading for Holiness," 48.
22. Casey, *Sacred Reading*, 9.

Contemplatio (contemplation)

Pennington[23] considers the etymology of "contemplation." Elements of the word include ancient Roman terminology concerning a segment of the heavens from which could be discerned the will of the gods; the sense of communion; and an abiding state. Pennington arrives at the following definition of contemplation: "to abide with God within his temple."[24]

Contemplatio, then, is to rest with and be with God with an enhanced sense of his presence. It is a state of awareness of God facilitated by the combined effects of having given attention to *lectio, meditatio* and *oratio*. Casey writes: "It can be said that the ultimate goal of *lectio divina* is contemplation. And according to the ancient way of viewing reality, the final aim of any project must stamp itself in each of the preliminary steps if any progress is to be made."[25] It is this stage of *lectio divina*, possibly more than any other stage, which depends most upon the gifts and grace of God. "Contemplation can never be seen as the outcome of a process. It remains a gift from God that is not automatically associated with particular human acts."[26]

Contemplatio – incarnate the text
- Rest in and be with God
- There can be an enhanced sense of his presence
- It is gift; it is grace
- It *must* lead to action in the world

23. Pennington, *Lectio Divina*.
24. Ibid., 65.
25. Casey, *Sacred Reading*, 60.
26. Ibid., 59.

Ignatian Contemplation

Of each preacher I would ask: Can you say that, like Ignatius, you have truly encountered the living and true God? Can you say that you know God Himself, not simply human words that describe Him? **WALTER BURGHARDT SJ**

The practice of contemplating the Gospels is but one aspect of a thirty-day retreat called the Spiritual Exercises. The Exercises developed out of Ignatius Loyola's (d. 1566) own spiritual conversion and journey and were subsequently used as the initial training for those called to the order Ignatius established: the Society of Jesus (Jesuits). The Exercises are structured into four weeks during which the life of Christ, as recorded in the Gospels, is contemplated. Each "week" is not necessarily a seven-day period; the duration depends on the progress of the retreatant.

While there are several types of prayer in the Exercises, the contemplations on the life of Jesus are the main activity. The retreatant contemplates the events in Jesus' life in chronological order. The Exercises begin in Week One by laying spiritual foundations for the retreat and include rigorous consideration of, and contemplation on, sin. Week Two focuses on the life and ministry of Jesus, Week Three on the passion and Week Four the resurrection. These contemplations are marked by the use of the five physical senses in imagining an event from Jesus' life as recorded in the Gospels. "Ignatian contemplation consists, then, in *reliving the mystery with a great deal of faith and love*; that is, the one who is praying relives the Gospel account as if he were present there and had a part to play in the unfolding mystery."[27]

No matter how cursory a person considers the Exercises, "[i]t is perfectly obvious from the very start that the Exercises are essentially a clearly defined method of contemplating the divine and human life of Christ on earth."[28] However, to fail to appreciate the place of these within the full orb of the Exercises is to reduce them to "a disconnected set of devout contemplations on the Gospel."[29] In an extended section written for the purpose of clarifying the nature of the Exercises, Rahner writes:

---

27. Ravier, *A Do-It-At-Home Retreat*, 39, emphasis in original.
28. Rahner, *Ignatius the Theologian*, 54.
29. Ibid.

The Exercises are never simply a series of meditations, nor even a summary of the spiritual life. Their meaning emerges only in the light of their ultimate purpose: to present the exercitant with a choice which transforms his life and in which he must find in peace the will of God for him by conforming himself, as far as he possibly can in his particular situation, to the law of life laid down by Christ.[30]

Thus, the Exercises are a means by which a person is presented with the presence and love of God and the challenge of how they will respond to the call of the King.

The manner of prayer contained in Gospel Contemplations that utilizes the physical senses was not original to Ignatius. It predated him by centuries; however, Ignatius' contribution was to rescue it from excess and place it within a more helpful context of other spiritual disciplines and theology.

---

30. Ibid., 55.

Selected Quotes Concerning Ignatian Contemplation

Imaginations differ, and we need to let God use the one we have and not bemoan the one we do not have.[31]

You must pray however you can and don't try to pray however you can't.
ADVICE GIVEN BY AN OLD ABBOT

The only way to get rid of misconceptions about contemplation is to experience it.[32]

The aim of the Exercises was to facilitate "contemplatives in action":

> Contemplativus in actione, *yes. But a more exact formulation of what Ignatius had in mind would be united to God in seeking and doing God's will. We are united to God not by prayer as such but by seeking and doing what God wants. Sometimes this means praying. More often it means some other kind of activity. A Jesuit told Ignatius that he found God primarily in solitude and by meditating or praying privately. Ignatius responded, "What do you mean? Do you draw no profit from helping your neighbor? For this is our practice."*[33]

The story of God's inner being is written everywhere, strewn around us like pearls in a parking lot, like love letters in a tip, like treasure hidden in every field. All we ask for is the grace to notice and believe in this extravagance, to identify the grace place. This is the work of contemplation.[34]

---

31. Barry, *Letting God Come Close*, 102.
32. Merton, *Seeds of Contemplation* (Hertfordshire: Anthony Clarke, 1972), 5.
33. Brackley, *Call to Discernment*, 245.
34. Daniel O'Leary, "Windows of Wonder," *The Tablet* (2008): page number unknown.

It may appear that the outline of Ignatian Contemplation is formulaic and marked by constraint. However, the Exercises are marked by freedom, generosity of spirit and an appreciation of individual preferences, circumstances and abilities of retreatants.[35] *While the contemplations are powerfully rooted in the Word, "what is striking throughout [the Exercises] is the liberty given to retreatants to allow their imagination full rein. There is no attempt whatsoever to control the retreatants' reflection through any biblical data not bearing immediately upon the purpose of the meditation."*[36] *Ignatius' own counsel to St Francis Borgia in this matter included the following: "God sees and knows what is best for us, and as he knows all, he points out the way to follow. But we, even with his grace, have a hard time finding it, and may have to try several ways before we travel by that which is evidently the one for us."*[37]

Contemplating Jesus' life is an imaginative exercise but not a fantasy. For believers, Christ is present in a way that Mozart and Joan of Arc are not. He lives among us through His Spirit. Working through our imagination, the Spirit communicates interior knowledge of Christ and sparks love for Him and His way of life.[38]

[Gospel Contemplation] can mould and change us in accordance with the word of God, and can reach our innermost hearts, the most fundamental attitudes and dispositions which day by day give shape and colour to our lives. This form of imaginative contemplation helps people to put on "the mind of Christ."[39]

Prayer is the work of God. His work in us. A sign that someone has contemplated is when they cannot say what happened or what they prayed for or about. When they answer that they prayed for this or that – it is not contemplation.[40]

---

35. Ravier, *Ignatius Loyola; A Do-It-At-Home Retreat*; Lonsdale, *Eyes to See, Ears to Hear.*

36. Byrne, "To See with the Eyes," 6.

37. Brou, *Ignatian Methods of Prayer*, 24.

38. Brackley, *Call to Discernment*, 75–76.

39. Lonsdale, *Eyes to See, Ears to Hear*, 114.

40. Fr John O'Connor, interview about Ignatian spirituality with the author, 2009.

The essence of Ignatius' message was "Wake up!" The Application of the Senses is about breathing!! We are not breathing!! We are not alive. Ignatius would say we draw on the five senses to be present. So that later after prayer we are present even to that person walking by who we would otherwise dismiss or ignore.[41]

People either live like angels and deny their humanness, or live like animals and indulge in it.[42]

The heart of Ignatius' approach was counter-cultural. He lived in a very religious era – but he preached Christ crucified.[43]

Preachers don't understand prayer. They might say their prayers but they are not abandoned to it all. Prayer expands our view – which is why we don't like it. It shows us possibilities. Imagination does not just involve the mind – it involves the whole body.[44]

---

41. Ibid.
42. Ibid.
43. Ibid.
44. Ibid.

Preparatory Prayer

To begin, a person quietens their heart and focuses on what is about to take place and why.[45] This involves consciously placing oneself in the presence of God and being aware of the love of God towards oneself.[46]

- Quieten your heart and prayerfully focus on what you are about to do.
- Be aware of the love of God towards you at this time.

---

45. Ravier, *A Do-It-At-Home Retreat.*
46. Brackley, *Call to Discernment.*

First Prelude: Subject Matter

This is basically an orientation of the subject matter as a whole. The following example is taken from the contemplation on the Last Supper (Matt 26:20–30; John 13:1–30):

> This is the history. Here it will be to recall that Christ our Lord sent two of His disciples from Bethany to Jerusalem to prepare the Supper, and afterwards, He himself went there with His disciples. After they had eaten the Paschal Lamb and supped, He washed their feet, and gave His most Sacred Body and Precious Blood to His disciples. When Judas had gone out to sell his Lord, Christ addressed His disciples.[47]

In the First Prelude the passage of Scripture is read and re-read so that the story is absorbed as much as possible.

———————————————

Read and re-read a story from Scripture (ideally a story from the Gospels)

———————————————

47. Puhl, *Spiritual Exercises of St Ignatius*, 64.

Second Prelude: Composition of Place

Then, relying on the description from Scripture, the imagination is used to compose the scene for contemplation. The five physical senses are employed to build the scene. In the Exercises Ignatius would provide brief prompts to excite the imagination. For instance, for the contemplation on the birth of Christ, he writes:

> This is a mental representation of the place. It will consist here in seeing in imagination the way from Nazareth to Bethlehem. Consider its length, its breadth; whether level, or through valleys and over hills. Observe also the place or cave where Christ is born; whether big or little; whether high or low; and how it is arranged.[48]

It is important to note that while liberty of expression is a feature of Ignatian spirituality, appropriate accuracy of the composition of place is salutary. "The composition of place should be made, so to say, in the spirit of prayer."[49] The elements of the place ought to be in harmony with the event and scene being imagined. For instance, while horror and despair would mark contemplation on the crucifixion, joy and wonder would mark contemplation of the resurrection.

Draw on the five physical senses
    What do you:
- See?
- Feel?
- Smell?
- Hear?
- Taste?

---

48. Ibid., 43.
49. Brou, *Ignatian Methods of Prayer*, 98.

Third Prelude: Asking for the Desired Grace

This is a prayer whereby a person entrusts himself or herself to the grace of God, asking, in the words of Ignatius, "for the grace that all my intentions, actions, and operations may be ordered purely to the service and praise of his Divine Majesty."[50] Throughout the Exercises the desired grace asked for could be "an intimate knowledge of our Lord"[51] or "sorrow, compassion, and shame because the Lord is going to his suffering for my sins."[52] The specific grace requested will vary from person to person and depend on the material being contemplated and on the current circumstances the person is experiencing.[53] It may appear that to ask for specific grace pre-empts and attempts to engineer the outcome of the prayer. However, it was recognized that it was one thing to request a particular grace but quite another as to how the Holy Spirit might answer that request. Ignatius' thinking was that to ask for grace was due to the influence of God in any case. He writes: "What I so much desire I shall not labour to obtain through my own effort, but I shall ask for it, because I know I can do nothing. Under the impulse of grace which makes me feel my need, I ask God to give me that which I cannot help desiring."[54] Thus the importance of the three preludes can be appreciated insofar as the Spirit of God is at work in this very process of preparation to contemplate.

Specifically ask for grace in keeping with the story or what is most pressing for you. For example, "I ask and I desire that I may know Christ more clearly, follow him more nearly and love him more dearly."

---

50. Puhl, *Spiritual Exercises of St Ignatius*, 21.
51. Ibid., 42.
52. Ibid., 63.
53. Brou, *Ignatian Methods of Prayer*.
54. Quoted in Brou, *Ignatian Methods of Prayer*, 104.

Contemplation

Once the person has been orientated to the Scripture at hand and the presence of God, the contemplation itself begins. Brackley puts it succinctly when he writes that we must "allow the story to unfold in our imagination like a film."[55] Once the contemplation commences "[w]e enter the story . . . considering above all the people involved: we (1) observe them, (2) listen to what they say, and (3) note what they do (not necessarily in that order), reflecting on what promises to bear fruit."[56] So a person enters the story and, in the same way as with poetry or a novel, allows their imagination to be touched by the biblical event.[57] Ignatius listed points which served as direction for the one praying. Such points could include who is to be in the contemplation, what to listen for or what to observe. A person can choose to be an observer or a participant as the story plays out in the imagination. As a participant, a person can adopt the place of one of the main characters in the story or simply inject themselves into the action.

Contemplate
- Choose to be a character or an observer.
- Run the story in your imagination like a movie.

If you wish to draw profit from these meditations . . . make everything that the Lord Jesus said and did present to yourself, just as though you were hearing it with your ears and seeing it with your eyes . . . And even when it is related in the past tense you should contemplate it all as though present today.
An unknown Franciscan in the fourteenth century

We let the words of a Gospel scene touch our imaginations much as poetry or a novel might, asking the Lord to reveal himself to us in the process. We can imagine ourselves as actually a part of the scene, as Ignatius suggests.
William A. Barry SJ

---

55. Brackley, *Call to Discernment*, 239.
56. Brou, *Ignatian Methods of Prayer*; Brackley, *Call to Discernment*.
57. Barry, *Letting God Come Close.*

True contemplation increases a person's presence and attentiveness to the presence and attentiveness of God in day-to-day life. Contemplation and action are not opposites but complementary.[58]

---

58. Brackley, *Call to Discernment.*

Colloquy

> At the end of the contemplation . . .
>
> . . . Speak with Jesus as "one friend speaking with another."

The contemplation finishes with a conversation or discussion with Christ regardless of how the contemplation is considered to have gone.[59] The subject for the colloquy is whatever has transpired in the preceding contemplation and the conversation is conducted "in the way one friend speaks to another, or a servant to one in authority."[60] Authenticity is crucial in the colloquy:

> In the colloquy I ought always to speak and pray according to the actual state of my soul. In other words, whether I am tempted or fervent, whether I want this virtue or that, whether I want to get ready to make a particular commitment, or whether I want to be sad or joyful in the mystery I am contemplating – the point is that I should never divorce my here-and-now self from my conversation in the colloquy.[61]

This form of imaginative contemplation helps people to put on "the mind of Christ".   DAVID LONSDALE

Contemplativus in actione
Both ways of praying address a "heresy" and "tragedy of church history":
- The loss of contemplation in everyday life
- The belief that contemplation belongs in monasteries and convents

---

59. Ravier, *A Do-It-At-Home Retreat.*
60. Brackley, *Call to Discernment*, 74.
61. Ravier, *A Do-It-At-Home Retreat*, 33, emphasis in original.

Definitions of Meditation and Contemplation

The words "meditation" and "contemplation" are often used interchangeably and definition can be difficult to nail down.[62]

> **Meditation** is a prayerful quest engaging thought, imagination, emotion, and desire. Its goal is to make our own in faith the subject considered, by confronting it with the reality of our own life.

> **Contemplative prayer** is the simple expression of the mystery of prayer. It is a gaze of faith fixed on Jesus, an attentiveness to the Word of God, a silent love. It achieves real union with the prayer of Christ to the extent that it makes us share in his mystery.

Meditation

Meditation is above all a quest. The mind seeks to understand the why and how of the Christian life, in order to adhere to and respond to what the Lord is asking.

Christians owe it to themselves to develop the desire to meditate regularly, lest they come to resemble the three first kinds of soil in the parable of the sower. But a method is only a guide; the important thing is to advance, with the Holy Spirit, along the one way of prayer: Christ Jesus.

Contemplation

What is contemplative prayer?

- St Teresa answers: "Contemplative prayer in my opinion is nothing else than a close sharing between friends; it means taking time frequently to be alone with him who we know loves us." Contemplative prayer seeks him "whom my soul loves." It is Jesus, and in him, the Father.
- Contemplation is a gaze of faith, fixed on Jesus. "I look at him and he looks at me." This focus on Jesus is a renunciation of self.

---

62. The following text is taken from US Catholic Church, ed., *Catechism of the Catholic Church* (New York: Doubleday, 1995), 713–715.

Bibliography

Barry, William A. *Letting God Come Close: An Approach to the Ignatian Spiritual Exercises.* Chicago: Loyola Press, 2001.

Beecher, Henry Ward. "The Power of the Imagination." In *Developing a Christian Imagination: An Interpretative Anthology*, edited by Warren W. Wiersbe, 215–221. Wheaton, IL: Victor, 1995.

Boersma, Hans. "Spiritual Imagination: Recapitulation as an Interpretative Principle." In *Imagination and Interpretation: Christian Perspectives*, edited by Hans Boersma, 13–33. Vancouver: Regent College, 2005.

Borda, Orlando Fals. "Participatory (Action) Research in Social Theory: Origins and Challenges." In *Handbook of Action Research: Participatory Inquiry and Practice*, edited by Peter Reason and Hilary Bradbury, 27–37. London: Sage, 2001.

Brackley, Dean. *The Call to Discernment in Troubled Times: New Perspectives on the Transformative Wisdom of Ignatius of Loyola.* New York: Crossroad, 2004.

Brooks, Phillips. *Phillips Brooks on Preaching.* London: SPCK, 1965.

Brou, Alexandre. *Ignatian Methods of Prayer.* Milwaukee: Bruce, 1949.

Brueggemann, Walter. "An Imaginative 'Or.'" In *A Reader on Preaching: Making Connections*, edited by David Day, Jeff Astley and Leslie J. Francis, 51–64. Aldershot: Ashgate, 2005.

Buechner, Frederick. *Wishful Thinking: A Theological ABC.* New York: Harper & Row, 1973.

Burghardt, Walter J. *Preaching: The Art and the Craft.* New York: Paulist, 1987.

———. *Long Have I Loved You: A Theologian Reflects on His Church.* New York: Orbis, 2000.

Byrne, Brendan. "'To See with the Eyes of the Imagination . . .': Scripture in the Exercises and Recent Interpretation." *The Way* 72 (1991): 3–19.

Canham, Elizabeth. *Praying the Bible.* 2nd ed. Cincinnati: Forward Movement, 2001.

Casey, Michael. *Sacred Reading: The Ancient Art of Lectio Divina.* Liguor, MO: Triumph, 1996.

Champion, Donna and Frank A. Stowell. "Validating Action Research Field Studies: PEArL." *Systemic Practice and Action Research* 16, no. 1 (2003): 21–36.

Church of the Province of New Zealand. *A New Zealand Prayer Book: He Karakia Mihinare o Aotearoa*. Auckland: Collins, 1989.

Cohen, Louis, Lawrence Manion and Keith Morrison. *Research Methods in Education*. 5th ed. London: RoutledgeFalmer, 2002.

Da Silva e Araujo, Emmanuel. "Ignatian Spirituality as a Spirituality of Incarnation." *The Way* 47, nos 1 and 2 (2008): 67–80.

Davis, Ellen F. *Imagination Shaped: Old Testament Preaching in the Anglican Tradition*. Valley Forge, PA: Trinity Press, 1995.

De Guibert, Joseph. *The Jesuits: Their Spiritual Doctrine and Practice – A Historical Study*. Chicago: Institute of Jesuit Sources, 1964.

De Verteuil, Michel. "Lectio Divina." Dominican Biblical Institute. Accessed 3 June 2009. http://www.dbclimerick.ie/lectiodivina.php.

De Vogue, Adalbert. *The Rule of Saint Benedict: A Doctrinal and Spiritual Commentary*. Kalamazoo, MI: Cistercian, 1983.

Dillon, Christopher. "Lectio Divina in the Monastic Tradition." *Cistercian Studies Quarterly* 34 (1999): 311–320.

Dwyer, Vincent. "Many Paths to Prayer: *Lectio Divina*." Accessed January 2015. http://www.jesuits.ca/orientations/dwyer.html#transcription.

Dysinger, Luke. "Accepting the Embrace of God: The Ancient Art of Lectio Divina." Valyermo Benedictine. Last modified 12 September 2005, accessed 3 June 2009. http://www.valyermo.com/ld-art.html.

Earle, Mary C. "The Process of Lectio Divina." *The Lutheran* 16 (2003): 24.

Egan, Keith J. "Guigo II: The Theology of the Contemplative Life." In *The Spirituality of Western Christendom*, edited by E. Rozanne Elder, 106–115. Kalamazoo, MI: Cistercian, 1976.

Endean, Philip. *Karl Rahner and Ignatian Spirituality*. Oxford: Oxford University Press, 2001.

Erikson, Millard J. *Christian Theology*. Grand Rapids: Baker, 1985.

Fiedler, Ernest J. "Lectio Divina: Devouring God's Word." *Liturgical Ministry* 5 (1996): 65–69.

Forbes, Cheryl. *Imagination: Embracing a Theology of Wonder*. Portland: Multnomah, 1986.

Gallagher, Michael Paul. "Newman on Imagination and Faith." First published 2002, accessed 30 October 2009. http://www.plaything.co.uk/gallagher/academic/newman_imagination.html.

————. "Theology and Imagination: From Theory to Practice." First published 2006, accessed 30 October 2009. http://www.plaything.co.uk/gallagher/academic/theol_imag.html.

Gasque, Laurel. "The Bible of the Poor: An Example of Medieval Interpretation and Its Relevance Today." In *Imagination and Interpretation: Christian Perspectives*, edited by Hans Boersma, 57–67. Vancouver: Regent College, 2005.

Goldingay, John. *An Ignatian Approach to Reading the Old Testament*. Cambridge: Grove, 2002.

————. "Premodern, Modern, and Postmodern in Old Testament Study." In *Eerdmans Commentary on the Bible*, edited by James D. G. Dunn and John W. Rogerson, 13–20. Grand Rapids: Eerdmans, 2003.

Green, Garret. *Imagining God: Theology and the Religious Imagination*. Grand Rapids: Eerdmans, 1989.

Greidanus, Sidney. *The Modern Preacher and the Ancient Text: Interpreting and Preaching Biblical Literature*. Grand Rapids: Eerdmans, 1988.

Guillen, Antonio. "Imitating Christ Our Lord with the Senses: Senses and Feeling in the Exercises." *The Way Supplement* 47, nos 1 and 2 (2008): 225–241.

Hall, Budd L. "I Wish This Were a Poem of Practices of Participatory Research." In *Handbook of Action Research: Participative Inquiry and Practice*, edited by Peter Reason and Hilary Bradbury, 171–178. London: Sage, 2001.

Heisler, Greg. *Spirit-led Preaching: The Holy Spirit's Role in Sermon Preparation and Delivery*. Nashville: B & H, 2007.

Heron, John and Peter Reason. "The Practice of Co-operative Inquiry: Research 'with' Rather Than 'on' People." In *Handbook of Action Research: Participative Inquiry and Practice*, edited by Peter Reason and Hilary Bradbury, 180–188. London: Sage, 2001.

Jones, Susan. "The Purpose of Preaching." *Candour* (2010): 10–11.

Kemmis, Stephen and Robin McTaggert. "Participatory Action Research." In *Handbook of Qualitative Research*, edited by Norman K. Denzin and Yvonna S. Lincoln, 567–605. 2nd ed. Thousand Oaks, CA: Sage, 2000.

Klein, William W., Craig L. Blomberg and Robert L. Hubbard Jr. *Introduction to Biblical Interpretation*. 2nd ed. Nashville: Thomas Nelson, 2004.

Ladd, George E. "The Search for Perspective." *Interpretation* 25, no. 1 (1971): 41–62.

Larsen, David L. *Telling the Old Old Story: The Art of Narrative Preaching.* Wheaton: Crossway, 1995.

Lischer, Richard. "Imagining a Sermon." In *A Reader on Preaching: Making Connections*, edited by David Day, Jeff Astley and Leslie J. Francis, 179–184. Aldershot: Ashgate, 2005.

Lloyd-Jones, Martyn. *Preaching and Preachers.* London: Hodder & Stoughton, 1971.

Loader, William. *The New Testament with Imagination: A Fresh Approach to Its Writings and Themes.* Grand Rapids: Eerdmans, 2007.

Long, Thomas G. "The Use of Scripture in Contemporary Preaching." *Interpretation* 44, no. 4 (1990): 341–352.

Lonsdale, David. *Eyes to See, Ears to Hear: An Introduction to Ignatian Spirituality.* Traditions of Christian Spirituality, edited by Philip Sheldrake. New York: Orbis, 2000.

Lynch, William F. *Images of Faith: An Exploration of the Ironic Imagination.* Notre Dame: Notre Dame Press, 1973.

———. *Images of Hope: Imagination as Healer of the Hopeless.* Notre Dame: Notre Dame Press, 1974.

MacDonald, George. *A Dish of Orts.* (Publishing details unknown), 1887.

McNiff, Jean, Pamela Lomax and Jack Whitehead. *You and Your Action Research Project.* 2nd ed. London: RoutledgeFalmer, 2003.

Merton, Thomas. *Opening the Bible.* Collegeville, MN: Liturgical Press, 1970.

———. *Seeds of Contemplation.* Hertfordshire: Anthony Clarke, 1972.

Miller, David L. "Lectio Divina Divine Reading." The Lutheran. December 2003, accessed 3 June 2009. http://www.thelutheran.org/article/article.cfm?article_id=3470.

Mulholland Jr., M. Robert. "Prayer as Availability to God." *Weavings* (1997): 20–26.

Newman, John Henry. *Grammar of Assent.* New York: Doubleday, 1955.

Nichols, J. Randall. *Building the Word: The Dynamics of Communication and Preaching.* San Francisco: Harper & Row, 1980.

Nieman, James R. "Preaching That Drives People from the Church." In *A Reader on Preaching: Making Connections*, edited by David Day, Jeff Astley and Leslie J. Francis, 247–254. Aldershot: Ashgate, 2005.

Northcutt, Kay L. *Kindling Desire for God: Preaching as Spiritual Direction.* Minneapolis: Fortress, 2009.

Nouwen, Henri. "Moving from Solitude to Community to Ministry." *Leadership* (Spring 1995): 81–87.

O'Connor, Fr. John. Interview about Ignatian spirituality with the author, 2009.

O'Donnell, Gabriel. "Reading for Holiness: Lectio Divina." In *Spiritual Traditions for the Contemporary Church*, edited by Robin Maas and Gabriel O'Donnell, 45–54. Nashville: Abingdon, 1990.

O'Leary, Daniel. "Windows of Wonder." *The Tablet* (2008).

Park, Peter. "Knowledge and Participatory Research." In *Handbook of Action Research: Participative Inquiry and Practice*, edited by Peter Reason and Hilary Bradbury. London: Sage, 2001.

Patton, Michael Quinn. *Qualitative Research and Evaluation Methods*. 3rd ed. Thousand Oaks, CA: Sage, 2002.

Pennington, Basil M. *Lectio Divina: Renewing the Ancient Practice of Praying the Scriptures*. New York: Crossroad, 1998.

———. *Who Do You Say I Am? Meditations on Jesus' Questions in the Gospels*. New York: New City Press, 2005.

Peterson, Eugene H. *Reversed Thunder: The Revelation of John and the Praying Imagination*. San Francisco: HarperSanFrancisco, 1988.

———. *Under the Unpredictable Plant: An Exploration in Vocational Holiness*. Grand Rapids: Eerdmans, 1992.

———. *Eat This Book: A Conversation in the Art of Spiritual Reading*. Grand Rapids: Eerdmans, 2006.

Puhl, Louis J., ed. *The Spiritual Exercises of St Ignatius*. Vintage Spiritual Classics. New York: Vintage Books, 2000.

Quicke, Michael. *360-Degree Preaching: Hearing, Speaking and Living the Word*. Grand Rapids: Baker, 2003.

Rahner, Hugo. *Ignatius the Theologian*. New York: Herder & Herder, 1968.

Rahner, Karl. *The Spirituality of the Church of the Future*. (Publishing details unknown), 1981.

———. *The Practice of Faith*. New York: Crossroad, 1986.

Ramsey, Boniface. "The Spirituality of the Early Church: Patristic Sources." In *Spiritual Traditions for the Contemporary Church*, edited by Robin Maas and Gabriel O'Donnell, OP, 25–44. Nashville: Abingdon, 1990.

Ravier, Andre. *Ignatius Loyola and the Founding of the Society of Jesus*. San Francisco: Ignatius Press, 1987.

———. *A Do-It-At-Home Retreat: The Spiritual Exercises of St Ignatius of Loyola*. San Francisco: Ignatius Press, 1991.

Reason, Peter. "Three Approaches to Participative Inquiry." In *Handbook of Qualitative Research*, edited by Norman K. Denzin and Yvonna S. Lincoln, 324–339. Thousand Oaks, CA: Sage, 1994.

Russell, Kenneth C. "Why Lectio Divina is Difficult." *Spiritual Life* 49 (2003): 67–75.

Schaer, Cathrin. "She's Right, Mate." *Canvas* (2006): 10–12.

Schneiders, Sandra. "Biblical Spirituality." *Interpretation* 56, no. 2 (2002): 133–142.

Smith, Neil Gregor. "Imagination in Exegesis." *Interpretation* 10, no. 4 (1956): 420–426.

Squire, Aelred. *Asking the Fathers*. London: SPCK, 1973.

Steinmetz, David C. "Luther and Loyola." *Interpretation* 47, no. 1 (1993): 5–14.

Stortz, Martha Ellen. *PastorPower*. Nashville: Abingdon, 1993.

Swinton, John and Harriet Mowat. *Practical Theology and Qualitative Research*. London: SCM, 2006.

Thurston, Bonnie. "On Biblical Preaching." *The Way Supplement* 48, no. 1 (2009): 67–80.

Tozer, A. W. "The Value of a Sanctified Imagination." In *Developing a Christian Imagination: An Interpretive Anthology*, edited by Warren W. Wiersbe, 211–214. Wheaton, IL: Victor, 1995.

Trainor, Michael. "Towards a Parish Spirituality of the Word of God." *Compass* 42, no. 4 (2008): 22–30.

Troeger, Thomas H. *Imaging a Sermon*. Nashville: Abingdon, 1990.

US Catholic Church, ed. *Catechism of the Catholic Church*. New York: Doubleday, 1995.

Von Balthasar, Hans Urs. *Essays in Theology II: Word and Redemption*. New York: Herder & Herder, 1965.

———. *The Glory of the Lord: A Theological Aesthetics. Vol. I, Seeing the Form*, edited by John Riches. Edinburgh: T & T Clark, 1982.

Wiersbe, Warren W. *Preaching and Teaching with Imagination: The Quest for Biblical Ministry*. Grand Rapids: Baker, 1994.

Windsor, Paul. "Introduction to Preaching." Course taught at Carey Baptist College, Auckland, 2005.

Wright, N. T. *Scripture and the Authority of God*. London: SPCK, 2005.

———. "Q and A with Bishop Wright on 'Justification.'" Ben Witherington on the Bible and Culture, Beliefnet. 2009, accessed 9 September 2010. http://blog.beliefnet.com/bibleandculture/2009/06/q-and-a-with-bishop-wright-on-justification.html.

Langham Literature and its imprints are a ministry of Langham Partnership.

Langham Partnership is a global fellowship working in pursuit of the vision God entrusted to its founder John Stott –

to facilitate the growth of the church in maturity and Christ-likeness through raising the standards of biblical preaching and teaching.

Our vision is to see churches in the majority world equipped for mission and growing to maturity in Christ through the ministry of pastors and leaders who believe, teach and live by the Word of God.

Our mission is to strengthen the ministry of the Word of God through:
- nurturing national movements for biblical preaching
- fostering the creation and distribution of evangelical literature
- enhancing evangelical theological education

especially in countries where churches are under-resourced.

Our ministry

Langham Preaching partners with national leaders to nurture indigenous biblical preaching movements for pastors and lay preachers all around the world. With the support of a team of trainers from many countries, a multi-level programme of seminars provides practical training, and is followed by a programme for training local facilitators. Local preachers' groups and national and regional networks ensure continuity and ongoing development, seeking to build vigorous movements committed to Bible exposition.

Langham Literature provides majority world preachers, scholars and seminary libraries with evangelical books and electronic resources through publishing and distribution, grants and discounts. The programme also fosters the creation of indigenous evangelical books in many languages, through writer's grants, strengthening local evangelical publishing houses, and investment in major regional literature projects, such as one volume Bible commentaries like *The Africa Bible Commentary* and *The South Asia Bible Commentary*.

Langham Scholars provides financial support for evangelical doctoral students from the majority world so that, when they return home, they may train pastors and other Christian leaders with sound, biblical and theological teaching. This programme equips those who equip others. Langham Scholars also works in partnership with majority world seminaries in strengthening evangelical theological education. A growing number of Langham Scholars study in high quality doctoral programmes in the majority world itself. As well as teaching the next generation of pastors, graduated Langham Scholars exercise significant influence through their writing and leadership.

To learn more about Langham Partnership and the work we do visit **langham.org**

Lightning Source UK Ltd.
Milton Keynes UK
UKOW06f0422110116

266105UK00003B/56/P